Gra for the Color Blue

SURVIVING THE LOSS OF
AN ADULT CHILD

Ellyn Wolfe

CAPE ANN PUBLISHING

Cape Ann Publishing
Gloucester, MA
gratefulforthecolorblue@gmail.com

Grateful for the Color Blue/Ellyn Wolfe 1st ed.
ISBN 978 -1-7349971-0-1

Contents

To Shannon

WHEN MY SON WAS dying, I looked everywhere for a book written by a parent who had lost her adult child. I hoped to find solace in the company of another who knew what I was going through, the horror I believed "outsiders" could not understand. I longed for someone who could look into my soul, know the intensity of my experience, and be compassionate.

I found nothing. Bookstores had shelves of material on the loss of young children and spouses, but nothing about losing adult children. I felt alone.

This memoir is my outreach to those who need to know they are not alone, that someone out there understands on a deep level and offers compassion and support through my words.

PART I

MASSACHUSETTS

Intuition

August 25, 2002   Annisquam, Massachusetts

MY INTUITION KICKED IN this morning with a message so clear it felt alive. "It's time for you to rekindle your relationship with your brother," it said and nothing more.

I've only had a couple serious instinctive hits like this across my lifetime. One wisely warned me to not get on an airplane. That was enough for me to realize, whatever it is, wherever it comes from, I need to pay attention and follow through.

Now my logical mind is racing to apply meaning, to find an explanation. I don't know what the future holds, but apparently it involves something big for my brother and me. Maybe it's related to the soul-searching I've been doing recently. If so, this will be a major piece. I'm ready to move forward in life with less baggage—baggage that has been weighing me down, like not seeing my brother for nineteen years.

CHAPTER 2

Reconnection

September 19, 2002   Portland International Airport, Oregon

WHEN I SEE HIM, I can't believe what my eyes are telling me. The signals my brain transmits are clear, but my mind is confused. I know I am seeing him, but it can't be—my dad, dead now, oh, over ten years, is grinning and waving at me as he moves close enough to throw his arms around me.

His bright blue eyes are mine. I feel as if I am looking back at myself. They're clear and deep, seeing more than the average set of eyes. He, too, is stunned and stares at me.

"I can't believe it," we both say at the same time.

"Mary and I figured it out last night. It's been 19 years."

"Nineteen years. How is it possible it could be that long? It's so good to be here and see you."

My brain finally catches up with my eyes. "You look just like Dad."

My brother Russell has evolved into my father as I remember him from so long ago. My brother is 60. I'm almost 54. How can that be? Aren't we both still kids?

He tells me on the drive home to be prepared because Mary keeps two small goats inside the house. "It's just something she does. I don't know. It's just Mary."

"Oh. Goats." My mind is prepared to accept anything because I don't know my brother or my sister-in-law. After so much time, what can I know? To cover my discomfort, I stretch a story and tell him how an animal-loving friend took care of a horse and a few geese this past winter and, on a particularly cold night, let them come into the house. (It was a section of the barn attached to the house, but I don't go there.)

"Same thing," he says.

"Don't they smell?"

"Sometimes, but I put up with it because she likes them."

Yikes.

As he opens the door to his home in the woods, he warns about the dog. "She's very protective, might take a bite. Be careful." Out pops the snout of a wiggly, smiling pooch, Sage, who will lay down her life for a scratch behind her ears and under her chin. Then I hear the laugh I remember from childhood when Russ would watch *Rocky and Bullwinkle* and laugh 'til there were tears. My brother is still a nut with a goofy sense of humor. There are no goats, no killer dog. We're both still kids inside. We laugh, and some reconnection tension eases up.

In their kitchen (the goatless kitchen), over the stove is a poster-sized photograph of our dad with Russ and Mary's only child, Russell Troy (RT to avoid father/son name confusion). They're sitting on the porch, arms draped over each other's shoulders, each looking as if life couldn't get any better. Seeing my dad again brings tears. He was such a good guy—gentle, kind, loved his kids, but couldn't express it. He expressed his love in the swing he made for us in the hawthorn tree, the wheelbarrow rides around the backyard, the doll clothes wardrobes with our names on the front that he built for me, my sister, and my three cousins who lost their own dad a few years before. Dad was pure of heart. Already I can see my brother appears to be so much like him.

How is it that Russ and I are old enough to have kids who are now adults? Time somehow stopped when I moved to Massachusetts, and he and Mary moved to Oregon. We lost touch. Can it be my kids, Rob and Shannon, are thirty-three and thirty, and RT is twenty-nine?

Growing up, my brother and I never got along. He's six years older and was the highly revered first-born male child. I was fussed over as the baby.

He squeaked through high school, then entered the printing trade when I was in fifth grade. There may have been a learning disability that accompanied his "to hell with education" attitude, but no one knew about those things in the Fifties. I loved school, loved that my teachers knew so much and wanted to share that knowledge with me. Driving to school early on a cold wintry morning with my dad, I remember feeling excited seeing Ben Franklin Elementary in the distance. Its windows blazed light and beckoned me to come join in and leave the cold and dark behind.

I couldn't wait to leave home for college and broaden my horizons beyond what I considered my limiting family with their old-fashioned views. Russell was all about tradition. He continued with the simple and familiar way of life we lived as children.

He choked me once, out by the apple tree just beyond the patio. It's one of those freeze-frame moments in my life when I was truly frightened and one of many reasons I kept a distance.

Our teen years boil down to two degrading labels—he referred to me as "The Socialite," and I called him "The Greaser."

As adults, what we wanted from life sent us in opposite directions, and not talking contributed to the distance. I've read about other families who have had spats over something insignificant, causing them to polarize, deepen the rift with time, and then pass the feud along to their children. How ridiculous they are. I judge them as if I haven't been doing the same thing.

After only a few hours of talking in his kitchen, I'm amazed at how differently I see him. In my mind Russell has evolved from the child I avoided, into a generous, sensitive, and fun-loving man. And maybe I have evolved too and can now see that he has always been this way, and it was our childhood struggles—my frustration at the special attention he had as the oldest and only boy in the family, and his frustration at the special attention I had as the baby—that colored our perspectives. As we trade stories over the next two days about ourselves and our children, the walls between us gently fall away, and a bond develops for the first time.

I fly home content with what we have achieved. But because of that intuitive message I got, part of me expected something more profound to happen. It didn't. We reconnected, and I finally have a relationship with my big brother. And that's enough.

The next eight months we carry on as normal siblings with phone calls, birthday cards, the usual. Little do we know this reunion is only groundwork for what is to come.

CHAPTER 3

Jolted

May 18, 2003   Annisquam, Massachusetts

I ROLL OUT OF bed at seven, grab a cup of peppermint tea, and
head outside to interact with Mother Nature, a deeply calm-
ing experience for me. I'm a Transcendentalist, in the style of
Emerson, Fuller, and Thoreau, who found their god and their
serenity in nature. My home is high on a granite ledge, nestled deep in the trees, and isolated from my neighbors who are
barely visible through the branches. My gardens, jumpstarted
by the wet spring, are a blaze of pink, yellow, and white blos-
soms. They usually invite me to sit among them and be still, but
this morning a multitude of unwelcome weeds have invaded
that seem to have appeared overnight.

As I pull the green intruders from the dirt and toss them
into the wheelbarrow, plans for an afternoon at the beach form
in my head. I imagine myself walking down Barberry Heights
Road, crossing Washington Street, and stepping down three
rough-hewn and mossy granite stairs into the narrow stretch
of woods along Lobster Cove. Emerging at the footbridge, I
stop to take in the antique homes nestled in the trees on the
other side, their faded colors reflecting in the rippling water.
I smile as I think about the kids who leap from the bridge rail-

ings into the water at summer's high tide, scramble onto the tiny floating dock, run up the ramp to where they started, and plunge in again and again. A short walk up the road is Annisquam, a tiny 18th Century village so small that when my urban friend from Boston and I took this same walk, and I said, "Here's downtown Annisquam," she looked around in all directions and said, "Where?"

"Ouch!" A thorn in my finger brings me sharply back to reality. My daydream sidetracks while I remove the barb, squeeze out a couple drops of blood, and try to shake the pain away. It hurts, but I carry on.

As the weed pile grows, I continue in my mind down the dusty path through the open field called Squam Rock Land Trust. I imagine stopping to check on the progress of the wild blueberries and to sniff the rosa rugosa along the tumbled down stone wall. At the crest of the hill, I stop to take in the Atlantic Ocean, the white shoreline of Wingarsheek Beach across the inlet, and the sailboat making its way past the lighthouse and out to sea.

Still daydreaming, I slip out of my sandals and let my feet sink into the cool, wet sand at the water's edge. Then I pick my way along the massive granite boulders that edge the beach until I reach my favorite, where I clamber up to the top. Depending on the tide, this self-proclaimed sanctuary is either a tiny island surrounded by chilly Atlantic waves, or an isolated lump sitting in the middle of damp sand and stones polished by eons of wave action. I visualize myself stretched out on the sun-warmed rock as the heat transfers into my back. I relax. My thoughts drift away.

The phone ringing in the house pulls me from my reverie. I rinse the dirt from my hands with the garden hose and dash for the kitchen.

"Hi, Mom."

My son's voice always brings a smile to my face when he calls each Saturday. Los Angeles is where he put down roots after graduating from USC with a degree in Theater Arts. He takes pride in having been a backstroker on the number one college swim team in the country and lives in unbridled joy in all aspects of his life. Rock climbing in Joshua Tree, swimming on a Master Men's team, playing guitar and singing in the band IRATIK (I'm Rob And This Is Keith) keep him happy. He writes song lyrics and is part of a tight group of actor-wannabe friends who call themselves The Core Four when they're all together and the Core Three without Rob. His brief hits of success sustain him as he pursues his acting career, but he supports himself by waiting tables at California Pizza Kitchen and selling mortgages while waiting for his big break in The Industry. Angel is his fiancée. They're planning a destination wedding in Prague next summer.

But today isn't Saturday. Why is he calling?

"Mom."

I hear him swallow hard and inhale deeply. Silence fills the next thirty seconds. I wait.

"Mom." His voice cracks. Is he crying?

"Rob, are you okay?"

"Mom, I have cancer."

My feet slide out from under me. My body does a slow descent against the kitchen wall until I hit the floor. Numb and speechless, my mind crashes into blackness. The world stops around me.

"W-w-hat?"

"I've been having what my doctor thought was acid reflux, but it hasn't gone away. They did an endoscopy yesterday and found a tumor in my stomach. Mom, it's the size of a baseball." He breaks into sobs at the same time I do. I gasp for breath, choking on my tears, lost in a surreal nightmare.

"Are they sure it's cancer? Tumors aren't always cancerous. They can be benign." I utter, hoping my optimism will somehow ease his fear and mine and magically influence the test results that haven't come in yet. He answers with something that sounds not very hopeful. My brain filters it out as I descend further into disbelief.

"How did this happen? How did it start? Is it only in your stomach? It hasn't spread, has it?" I ask, panicked. "Are you okay? I mean, I know you're not okay. Well, maybe you're okay. You will be okay. Right?"

Questions rapid fire out of me, searching for the answer that tells me this will be an easy fix, that there is nothing to fix because it will be benign. "Who's your doctor? What are his credentials? Do you want to come back to Boston for a second opinion? Mass Gen is one of the best in the country."

Crazy thoughts ricochet through my head. Maternal instincts are in full fight-or-flight mode. My entire body shakes. My son. How can I protect him? How can I help make it go away?

"I wish I could hold you and you me right now. Oh, my god. Rob."

"Mom." He eases back into temporary control. "We don't have the final test results yet. My doctor was trying to be optimistic yesterday, but I could tell he was shaken by what he saw in there. He'll call me as soon as he knows for sure. Then I'll call you, and we'll start to figure things out."

"Please let me know the second you get the results. Call me at work. It's okay to interrupt me. I'll tell Susan to find me if I'm not at my desk. I love you so much, Rob." I'm not sure what else we say, but we cry a lot. 'Mom, I have cancer' has seared into my brain and taken me hostage.

Immobile, I sit for at least an hour, my head back against the cabinets, my legs splayed on the cool tile floor in my little kitchen, listening to the clock's tick, tick, tick. In between each tick, my thoughts race to irrational extremes—awfulizing a death scenario one moment, then slamming the lid on that and heading in the opposite direction, imagining a diagnosis with pink clouds and sunshine and Tums as the easy solution.

Fearful of losing my sanity, I peel myself off the floor just enough to reach the phone. I call my daughter. "I'm leaving now," she says. "I'll be there in forty-five minutes."

I'm grateful she's coming. I need someone to hold on to, someone rational who can help me deal with this. I call my sister, my brother, my ex-husband/Rob's dad. This is not anything to share with my mother, whose Alzheimer's causes her enough difficulty with her own reality. I make my way out to the garden and sit, lost among the silent flowers and weeds.

The Bomb

May 19, 2003   Boston, Massachusetts

A DISTANT BUZZ YANKS me partially out of a dream. I can't make sense of where I am. Sleep finally came in the wee hours, dawn much too close on its heels. I get up, shower and dress, manage to put on shoes that match, make the train with two minutes to spare, then sit for one hour among the commuters, looking out the window, but seeing nothing. I jump when the conductor asks for my pass.

I hide out in my office and flinch each time the phone rings. I get rid of callers fast or send them to Susan to handle. A friend brings lunch so I can stay close to my phone. She distracts me with conversation, but I have trouble following her words. My trips to the ladies' room take only seconds, followed by a dash back to my desk. Susan, my admin extraordinaire, watches over me and covers for my vapid behavior.

At two o'clock Rob calls. "I have the results." He hesitates. When I hear him trying to gain control, hear the falter in his voice, I know.

"The tests are positive. It's cancer, Mom. The doctor called it adenocarcinoma." He pauses. "And he says it's aggressive."

Neither one of us speaks or breathes for what seems like a long time as the enormity sinks in. Then the emotions surge. "No-o-o!" I shout, and hysterical gasps for air mixed with sobs consume me. "Oh my god. No. Please. No." My senses are acute, but I am physically paralyzed. Typical panic syndrome. If I could squeeze myself into the phone and emerge in his apartment in LA, I would do it.

Through my office window, I see Susan's shoulders quiver. Her head drops low. She hears me through my closed door. I think everyone for several offices down hears me.

"What happens next?"

"Surgery." Rob says, the word catching in his throat. "And it will have to be soon. Mom. They're going to remove my stomach." He sucks in a sharp breath. "Or parts of my stomach. They won't know if it has spread until they're in there. Angel and I have appointments over the next five days to interview surgeons. Angel's sister works at John Wayne Cancer Institute in Santa Monica. She's a big help in getting us going in the right direction. Angel's on it big time."

I feel a million miles away and helpless. I manage Work/Life programs and policies for over 50,000 employees at one of the largest banks in the country. That seems like a cinch compared to this. I truly do not know what to do, how to proceed, or how I even fit into the healing picture.

"I'm coming. I'll be there tonight," I say.

"No, Mom. Not yet. Wait until we have more answers, until we figure out what we're going to do. That will probably be a few days. I want you here for my surgery, but Angel and I have to work out the details. I'll let you know as soon as I can."

There comes a time when suddenly you know life has gone by too quickly, and you have not noticed the changes around you. Because he has been on the West Coast for ten years, I only see Rob once, maybe twice, per year. I no longer know the day-to-day details of his life, just the conversational things. "I got a lead in a play. Will you come see me?" Or, "Look for me next Saturday night on the TV series ___. I walk past Garth Brooks and say, 'Nice hat.'" Or, "I met my future wife."

In my mind, I am still the mom of the pre-college Rob, the one he sought out to fix things. Somehow, I have failed to adjust my understanding of my reduced importance in his life. I have not really noticed that it has changed since Angel came into the picture four years ago. It's like hanging onto that old dress in the closet, the one that was so terrific many years ago, but is now out of date and needs to go to Goodwill. With this conversation, I begin to wake up to the fact that my momness has moved from an active identity to a passive one.

Angel calls me back ten minutes later. "I really want you to come tonight if you can. Rob is a wreck, and I think having his mom here would be the best thing for him."

I fly into action, get myself on the airline standby list for that evening, email my manager that I will be away, and ask Susan to step in and take over for me. I hold a strong belief that a good administrative assistant is totally capable, is usually one or two steps ahead of her manager, and is part of a company-wide network of assistants who are the only ones who really know what's going on in the organization.

I leave work immediately, fidget on the train ride home, throw clothes into a suitcase, and get myself back to the airport for an 8:40p.m. departure.

My dear friend Ginger, a career airline employee, gave me her American Airlines Companion Pass only months ago. What seemed like a fabulous treat turns into a godsend, a way for me to fly standby on any available seat at the drop of a hat. This feels more like the drop of a mega-bomb.

CHAPTER 5

A Surreal Visit

May 19, 2003   Flying to Los Angeles, California

ONCE ON THE PLANE, I have time to step back and try to make some sense of this. Children don't get fatal illnesses. They don't die before their parents. I try to grasp the enormity of what life has dumped on Rob and those who love him. I feel physically nauseated as the reality continues to seep in.

I'm not one to keep my feelings or my situations to myself. If I feel it, I share it. It's somewhat of a survival mechanism. I have a sweater with a red fabric heart stitched to the upper left sleeve, an apt metaphor for my communication style.

My first email, composed over Kansas, launches as we land at LAX.

My dear friends,

Bad news. I'll just say it—Rob was diagnosed with stomach cancer. I don't have any more information except that surgery will be soon, it will be in LA, and it will be intense. Once they get inside, they will remove his stomach and will find out if it has spread.

I'm sick with worry. I'm on my way to LA right now for a quick visit, then will return to LA as soon as Rob and

Angel find the right surgeon. I'll keep you all updated as best I can. Please send healing thoughts his way.

Love, Ellyn

May 20, 2003   Studio City, California

WE SIT AT ROB and Angel's dining table over a lunch we barely touch. I position myself across from Rob, Angel to his left. Over his shoulder and out the window I let my eyes rest for a moment on the pale yellow stucco apartment buildings with their neatly manicured lawns and gardens on the other side of Tujunga Street. I wonder what the inhabitants are talking about and long for the innocence of discussing last night's movie or the new show at the Getty Museum.

The brilliant California sunlight reflects off the windows and highlights the flower beds, which lightens my mood. But only for a second. I am painfully aware of the contrast between the light outside and the darkness within. Cancer is the shadowy intruder at our table, silently consuming spirits and flesh.

So many of Rob's and my conversations over the years focused on activities and plans, funny stories, news to celebrate, or small problems to solve. Pleasant talk, light in nature, but typical for families with children who have become adults and now live some distance away. Today's conversation is different.

"Rob, I don't get it." I said. "Where did this cancer come from? Do they have any idea what caused it?"

Farfetched possibilities have been racing through my head—too much chlorine from years of swim practice at the Weston High School, the Gloucester Y, and the USC pools? The suspected carcinogenic emissions from the Salem Power Plant that drift across Salem Sound to Manchester-by-the-Sea, our former neighborhood? What about that small sign in the apartment building's garden outside Rob and Angel's living room window that reads, "Chemicals used in this garden are known to cause cancer," which mysteriously disappeared when word of his diagnosis got out. Perhaps if we know what started it, that information will help the doctors end it. Determining an outside source will also calm my lurking parental guilt. Maybe something I did along the way was the cause? Oh god, I hope not. This is bad enough, but that would be the end of me.

"Not sure what they know or don't know about the cause," Rob answered. "The profile for stomach cancer is over 55 and Asian. It sure doesn't fit me." His face pale, his usual engaging smile, now a tight straight line, is almost a grimace. The joy has drained out of this lively soul, my son, my firstborn.

As I let my mind venture into the worst-case scenario, I feel sickened with the possibility of losing him. I don't know Rob's view on death. We've never talked about it. I steady myself and proceed. "I've done a lot of reading over the years, some of it on a spiritual level. My belief is that life goes on after death. The soul survives. I believe the body is a temporary home for the spirit in this lifetime. What about you, Rob? What do you think happens?"

"I think life is like a light switch. It's on, and you're alive. When it's off, that's it. There is nothing more." His voice is edgy, and he changes the subject quickly. Clearly, he doesn't want to talk about it anymore, which proves to be the case as time rolls on. Rob always maintains a positive outlook. He does not venture into the dark side. I suspect that's what makes him such an awesome competitor. He visualizes himself winning the race, sprinting across the pool and touching the wall first. That's exactly how he will handle this cancer. There is no question in his mind there is only one outcome, he will be the victor in this race toward survival. His switch will remain solidly on.

"We're going to postpone the wedding for a year." Angel pulls the conversation in another direction. "Rob should be recovered by then, and we'll all head to Prague for the ceremony. They have agreed to hold our deposit at this cool Fifteenth Century venue. What an awesome double celebration it's going to be!" Angel has the go-for-it attitude deeply ingrained as well. She will do all she can to make sure that switch stays on.

CHAPTER 6

Sanctuary

May 22, 2003   Annisquam, Massachusetts

BACK HOME IN ANNISQUAM, I sit on my deck in the treetops, a private sanctuary surrounded by dense leaf cover from many hundred-year-old oak trees. The ground slopes dramatically away from the back of the house, leaving me on a compatible level with the birds and their carefully constructed nests. In early autumn, falling acorns hammer this refuge day and night. I'm fond of these missiles with their little brown caps and dub them "acorn bombs" as they startle me out of reverie and sleep. Last September, one such bomb hit the tabletop just right and shattered the glass into tiny pieces. What a mess as I crawled under the deck to remove the shards so the resident ground hog wouldn't get hurt as he foraged for grubs.

A spiral staircase leads from this deck to another one on the roof, my favorite summer breakfast spot, a place to go when I truly want to get above it all. This little retreat sits above the canopy of trees, looking out to the Atlantic Ocean to the north, the Jones River to the west, neighbor Mike's house to the south, and a solid wall of trees to the east. Up here I feel lighter, less burdened by life's problems. It's as if I'm closer to the Higher

Powers and can feel the Big Plan is working as it should, not as I want it to.

The climb up the stairs seems too strenuous today. I need to feel more anchored, closer to the earth. I'm seated at my re-glazed table with one of my journals. The gentle spring sunshine dapples through the new tree leaves, speckling the pages.

I'm experimenting with multiple journals, each one a home for a specific topic, an attempt at an uninterrupted flow of thoughts, feelings, and ideas. Today I have North Shore Thoughts, a beautifully bound leather book (every now and again I stop and sniff the cover and sigh) with handmade paper pages, the kind of gift one puts on a shelf to save for someday special. I started writing in this one in 2001, a test for me to see if I could get beyond my crazy idea of saving things. For when? For what? I realized my life could be over before this beautiful journal even got started, so I plunged in. I used a special pen, which I had also been saving, purchased on a ten-day travel adventure in Hong Kong.

I try to disown some of my ugly and terrifying thoughts and hide them carefully away rather than write them down. But thoughts have a way of leaking out when I relax and let my guard down. Sitting here in the treetops, my guard slips silently away. Cancer is a killer. Rob has cancer. For the moment he has cancer. By next week's end I pray he will be cancer-free, enriched for having had the experience and having moved beyond it and back into living life to its fullest.

Cancer, in my mind, is something that happens to others, to the elderly, to those who have been living badly. All mythical thinking. Rob's illness is a reality I have a hard time grasping.

My son, Robert Mulloy the Great, as he signed one of his letters from summer camp years ago, has stomach cancer. Adenocarcinoma. Sounds dreadful. Is dreadful. My mind is like the stock market when it moves to avoid catastrophe—it shuts down. I can only grasp bits of reality when something powerful cracks open the steel door I've closed on it. The stuffed emotions leak out through my tears. I can't imagine what it's like for him.

When the reality gets too close, I move. I get busy. I find some way to either get myself involved in something or meditate to escape the pain. It works pretty well. As I sit here thinking about Rob, I'm aware of something strong beginning to tingle deep inside, something I recognize as a precursor to a full-blown emotional explosion. Time to move.

I grab my journal, pen, a bottle of water and take a brisk walk to the beach, to my favorite rock, my sanctuary by the sea. A friend calls it the Church of the Rocks. Walking mindfully pulls me away from the threat of inner turmoil and gets me focused on how the muscles in my legs feel, how my foot touches the ground heel first followed by toes, and how my arms pump back and forth as I ramble up and down the hills. I notice my other senses activating. The perfume of the woods makes the little hairs in my nose tickle, the tree branches clack musically in the breeze, and a gulp of water refreshes me as it passes over my tongue and down my throat. My sixth sense kicks in. There is peace waiting for me in my sanctuary.

It's my first visit to the beach this year. I'm exhilarated from my walk, and my Transcendentalist self is fully at one with the beauty of nature. As I climb up onto my favorite boulder, my eyes scan for the perfect spot to sit.

Strangely enough, this granite rock feels soft to me when I settle in. I get comfortable as I gaze out over the Atlantic, the sun sparkling on the gentle waves like so many jittering white diamonds. The glow of the sun creates a watery road that leads directly to my haven. The air is warm on my skin. My breathing slows, becomes rhythmic. I focus on my breath traveling in through my nose and down into my lungs, my belly gently expanding to make room for more. I observe as my belly draws in, the breath moves up from my lungs, and exhales gently out through my mouth. My posture straightens softly, and I gradually melt into a meditative state. This is the first time in a long time. My thoughts stop wandering for a moment or two. When they take off, I gently bring them back with no judgment. Brains are designed to wander. The mindful part of this practice is being aware that I am distracted, then bringing my attention back to my steady breathing.

This moment is all there is for right now, and I'm aware of myself in it. It will pass, then the next moment will be all there is. And so on. I'm not re-living my past. I'm not planning or fearing the future. I'm here on this rock, breathing, being. I'm part of the flow of nature. All things in the universe are connected and equally important. Nature has perfect balance. Carl Sagan said if you take one atom out of the universe, the whole universe will collapse. The total calm I feel right now helps me find a larger perspective on life. I can see from a higher level there are gifts in crisis.

An event of this magnitude, Rob's cancer, forces me to stop and reconnect with who I am. I am someone in distress who needs support and love. Could this be the first time that I'm letting myself receive help and kindness? I've always been the giver, the let-me-help-you person who puts her hand up in refusal when someone offers help. "Thanks, but no thanks. I'm fine. I'll be okay." I've taught classes on the art of giving and receiving, but it's only now that I really understand the depth of its meaning. By letting myself accept help and kindness from others, I'm allowing others to give. This creates balance, completes the circle of giving and receiving. It's what the world and I need desperately right now.

CHAPTER 7

Mothers

May 23, 2003   Annisquam, Massachusetts

DISEASE OF A SERIOUS and life-threatening nature is the ultimate tool, incentive, and motivator in giving one total focus. Often, I come home from my workday scattered, exhausted, distracted. I usually complain about my manager, the workplace, and a bevy of stress-producing scenarios, but Rob's illness and his ensuing measures to save his life have washed away all else as petty. When I was in LA with him, I had laser-like focus. Only one thing was important—Rob.

Mothers come with natural protective internal wiring that kicks in when a knee gets scraped from a bicycle spill, the third strike is called, or a bully makes your child cry. All had been activated over the years, but there comes a time after your child makes his way through college, finds the future Mrs. Mulloy, and is off living his life on the other side of the country and doing rather nicely, when the maternal instinct takes a well-deserved break and rests in semi-retirement somewhere in the tropical island recesses of the mind. A mom is always ready to take action by lending a sympathetic ear or offering parental wisdom, but for the most part, its piña colada time. However, when the phone rings and your grown child tells you his life is at risk, that retired instinct roars up inside ready to do battle and obliterate that evil bully and make the bad go away.

When I was in LA, Rob and Angel told me they would take the lead in getting Rob healed, that I could relax and not have to worry about being involved in making any medical choices.

"Your opinion is always welcome," they said, but they very kindly asked me to take a back seat. This was a shocking moment. I had an inkling from an earlier conversation, but now I shudder with the stark realization that I am no longer a decision-maker in his life. Yes, my opinions are welcome. However, those opinions are his to accept or decline. Nor am I the main woman in Rob's life anymore. Angel is.

Part of me is relieved. It seems strange to say it, but I feel pounds melt off my shoulders. This is a moment of profound role shifting. I take off my hat as mother superior in my son's life. No doubt it is a relief for him as well.

Angel, a fast-rising star in LA's male-dominated human computer interaction design industry and oh-so-smart, is organized and fastidious in her research. Rob scored in the 99th percentile on all those intelligence tests they do on kids in elementary and high school. He was the only member of the prestigious USC Swim Team with an academic, not sports, scholarship. I trust their judgment. Besides, I am three thousand miles away and feel powerless. If they lived in Boston, I have all sorts of connections and information, but in LA, nothing. All I can do is love them and support the huge decision they are about to make together.

CHAPTER 8

Reality

May 26, 2003   Boston, Massachusetts

I JUMP FOR THE phone when it rings, eager for any piece of news. Rob's voice is steady and decisive as he gives me details about the doctor he and Angel have selected at the John Wayne Cancer Institute, fifteen minutes away from their Studio City apartment when traveled at 5 a.m., two hours during LA rush hour. Dr. B is an innovative (I'm trying not to say cutting-edge) surgical oncologist specializing in gastric cancers. What sets him apart from the other world-class doctors they interviewed? He studied gastric surgical methods in Japan, where this type of stomach cancer is more prevalent. An excellent choice. Follow-up chemo will be at the USC Norris Comprehensive Cancer Center with Dr. L, an oncologist involved in the latest genetic-oncology research. Plus, Rob likes the USC connection.

Because the doctor identified Rob's cancer as aggressive and possibly traveling, he schedules radical surgery quickly, only three days from now on May 29. He will remove Rob's stomach, most of his esophagus, area lymph nodes, and maybe his spleen. I am sickened thinking about it.

Only a mother knows the intense connection between her body and her child's. Nine months of growing that little soul inside, creating a life from my own in which every bodily system is actively participating, connects us forever in an unbreakable bond. His cells are my cells. I feel his pain.

I mentally send a thank you to Ginger for my Companion Pass as I list myself once again on the airline standby list, this time for a Wednesday flight, the day before his operation. I hope to get on the first departure of the day, which usually means a first-class seat and a mimosa.

May 28, 2003   Flying to Los Angeles, California

THE MIMOSAS ARE GREAT. Even though I'm having two (okay, maybe three) and feel very relaxed on the plane, the intensity of what lies before Rob cuts through the dulling effect of alcohol and keeps me alert. Rob and Angel meet me at the baggage claim, where we exchange deep hugs while the carousel deposits suitcases behind us. Our moods are tense underneath, but stoic with a hint of cheer on the surface. We head straight to Santa Monica for a pre-surgery meeting with Dr. B.

On the way, they tell me about last night's party, which they refer to as The Last Supper. Close friends gathered at Vermont, their favorite restaurant where Rob proposed to Angel last year. (He had the waiter drop the engagement ring in her glass of champagne, with some trepidation that she might not notice it and, oh-my-god, swallow the ring.) This was a send-off dinner and a gustatory indulgence for a young man who loves a good meal and was about to lose his stomach.

Walking into the medical center lobby, I am stunned to see a life-size portrait of The Duke, outfitted in full Western gear with the signature bandana around his neck and a six-shooter resting on his hip. *What the heck is John Wayne doing in a doctor's office?* is my immediate thought, until I make the obvious connection. Next to the portrait is a quote: "Courage is being scared to death but saddling up anyway." His movie star status is what my brain remembers, forgetting it was stomach cancer that took him out. This place, The John Wayne Cancer Institute, providing world-renown oncologists to help others, is his legacy.

Sitting across the desk from Dr. B is like sitting in front of Jesus Christ as he plans his next miracle. Rob and Angel cling to each other, keenly focused on every word from the man who holds Rob's life in his hands. I sit in awe, staring at his hands, trying to imagine how they will maneuver the scalpel tomorrow. Silently I send prayers out to the universe that this man's knowledge and intuition will know exactly the right moves to make with it.

His voice is gentle yet strong, drawing us in with a compassionate manner and professional confidence. During the hour we sit with him, his eyes never leave ours. Trust. He conveys trust, and we feel it.

He reviews Rob's records with us, explains the intended procedure, and answers our endless questions. Before we leave, he cautions us. "Be prepared for a bout of serious illness but stay positive. You will no doubt search for information, but please don't get caught up in statistics. There are a lot of negative data out there. Each case is unique. Remember, Rob is young, strong, and otherwise healthy."

Of course, we have all scoured the internet already and are alarmed by the dreadful survival statistics we found.

CHAPTER 9

Surgery

May 29, 2003   St. John's Hospital. Santa Monica, California.

WE LEAVE ROB AND Angel's apartment in five a.m. darkness. Check-in for surgery is at seven. Silently we walk to the car, holding hands, afraid to say anything that might cause Rob's fear level to rise any higher than it already is. His terror is palpable. I am trying to block what I heard earlier—that Dr. B's patient survival rate on the table is 97%. My mind goes straight to the 3%. I suspect the same thing is going through Rob's and Angel's minds.

Once on the freeway, Angel breaks the silence. She tells me they have a Healthcare Power of Attorney in place, and they decided she will be the agent.

"We want to tell you before Rob goes in, in case anything happens. We were afraid it might hurt your feelings that we chose me as the decision maker and not you. We don't want you to feel slighted, but Rob and I are so connected and deeply involved in the details of all this, it seems the right thing to do."

"I understand completely," I answer. "I know you are the right one for this. I'm his mom, but you are the one he relies on. You two have a deep commitment to each other. I'm here to love Rob, to be with him while you're at work, and to help where needed day to day. You made the right decision."

Angel breathes a sigh of relief.

We arrive early, afraid the unpredictable LA traffic might have held us hostage. Rob is a wreck, not sure if this will be his last day on earth or not. Waiting only intensifies the panic. It's time for me to hand over the contents of the large bag I have been carrying.

Shannon, Rob's sister in Boston, feels helpless like so many of us. She wanted to do something to let him know she cares. Their relationship has been rocky since the day she was born. Rob had been the star, the one and only child and grandchild, the center of attention for three years until, in his mind, this little intruder came along and stole the limelight. He never got over it. In his mid-twenties, after they had some minor conflict, he glared at me and said angrily, "Why did she have to be born?"

Startled, I replied, "Rob, she's your sister. She's a good person, and she's not going away. It's time you got over it." I gave him the raised eyebrow, open-eyed look down my nose, indicating his comment was not only inappropriate, but ridiculous.

Before I left Annisquam for this second very important trip to LA, Shannon spent a few days at my house taking care of me, knowing I was scared. I loved having her nearby. One day she located stacks of my empty photo albums and boxes of loose photographs, carried them to the den, and plopped them on the carpet. She settled herself next to the piles, rifled through the boxes, then began to pull pictures out. She placed them in some sort of circular order around her.

"What are you doing?" I asked. She had been at it a while and looked like a small atoll floating in a sea of images.

"You'll see. Now leave me alone please," she said, offering nothing more. Shannon is my quiet child. She never talks about what is going on until it's finished, then she springs it on us. Like when she was in high school and waltzed into the kitchen one night, excited. "I got the part of Kolenkhov in the school play, *You Can't Take It With You*." She never mentioned auditioning. Who knew she was even interested in acting? Very different from her brother and me, who get everyone involved from the very beginning, whether they want to be or not.

Several hours later, she appeared in the kitchen with a photo album.

"I found this empty one. I hope it's okay that I used it." She laid her work on the table. "I made a book of happy memories for Rob. Each photo is something to make him smile. And he can tell Angel the stories behind the pictures. It's for him to look at before he goes into surgery. I figured he could use something to lighten up."

Her thoughtful gift works like magic. Angel's mouth falls open with amazement when she sees it. Rob scowls. He is ready to reject anything from his sister, but Angel opens to the first page and squeals with delight when she sees baby Rob in his father's arms, swaddled in blue blankets, a dandelion tucked behind his ear. Within minutes, they're huddled together on the waiting room couch, laughing. The next hour speeds by as Rob, a natural storyteller, recounts tale after tale, filling Angel in on his life before he met her and re-experiencing the joy of the life he has lived.

When the nurse comes for Rob, he has been so lost in the photos he temporarily forgets where he is. We hug like we never want to let go, and we kiss, knowing it could be our last. The "I love yous" are deep. He walks off reluctantly. The lightness of the past hour falls away, and fear takes its place.

A staff member escorts Angel and me to the surgical waiting room. Rows of semi-comfortable chairs filled with worried-faced bodies line up across the sunlit room. The clock ticks loudly on the wall behind the check-in desk. The receptionist tells us the surgeon will call during the five- to six-hour procedure to let us know how it is going.

"We have a nice cafeteria down the hall," she says. Looking into our eyes, she offers knowingly, "Try to relax. He's in good hands." I choose a seat in the back corner by the windows where I can be alone with my thoughts and prayers. Angel sits in the front row, close to the receptionist's phone.

Time flies when you're having fun and doesn't when you're not. During the first hour, my eyes drift up to the clock at least twice every minute. It seems as if its batteries are fading, and time has slowed to a near halt. It only gets worse as the morning wears on.

The desk phone finally rings at 11:30 a.m. "Mrs. Mulloy?" the receptionist announces. Both Angel and I stand up. Neither one of us is currently Mrs. Mulloy. I was years ago. Angel is about to be. We both start for the phone. I stop, remembering about the back seat, but my maternal instinct drives me ahead toward the phone. I take it, leaving Angel looking startled behind me. I am so keyed up that I cannot comprehend what Dr. B is saying. I interrupt him. "Wait a minute, please. I believe you want Angel." I hand the phone to her with a look of contrition, realizing I really am in the back seat.

Angel listens, asks questions, hangs up, then takes me aside in the crowded room. "Dr. B says, 'Rob is stable and doing well. All critical lymph nodes are removed, and stage one of the surgery is complete. Next stage is to go after the stomach and decide how much of the esophagus needs to be removed.'"

"Oh, thank god! What a relief to know he's okay so far!" I hesitate, then add, "Angel, I'm sorry. I realize you are the one who needs to be in charge. I ..."

"Don't apologize. You're his mom. Let's just get through this together." Angel is great at putting people at ease. Even though I am almost her mother-in-law, I know she loves me. She confessed months earlier—if she could have chosen two moms when she came into this world, I would have been one of them.

Little by little, the room empties of strangers. A flock of Angel's relatives arrive at noon with food, drink, and hugs, then settle in to wait with us. I have not left my seat at the back of the room since right after Dr. B's phone call, when I made a quick dash to the bathroom, afraid I might miss another update from the operating room. I don't talk with anyone and am too distracted to read, so I just sit there, my exterior numb, my interior in full panic attack. The clock creeps toward four p.m. What's taking so long? Dr. B said this would take five hours. That deadline was three hours ago. Why no more phone calls? I feel like a rocket ship just before take-off, the engines revving, countdown ticking off, hugely anxious about launching or blowing up.

The desk phone rings at 4:30. I stand up, but this time I sit back down and let the other Mrs. Mulloy take it. Angel listens carefully, asks some questions, hangs up. She turns and announces through a grin, "Dr. B says surgery is finished, and Rob is in good shape. The area around the organ removal is cancer free. Rob is 'rock solid and all cancer is out!'"

At the words, "all cancer is out," I leap out of my chair with a loud whoop that causes the remaining heads in the room to turn. Then I burst into tears with uncontrolled sobs, letting the rocket fuel launch me into near delirium. "He's cancer free!" I shout. Angel and I crumple into each other, holding onto life.

Dr. B meets with Angel and me post-surgery. He bursts into the room, pumped up by the complex and innovative procedure he has performed on Rob—removing his stomach, saving the spleen, using part of his colon to replace the section of his esophagus where the cancer had spread. He is sure this will be published in medical journals. I have mixed thoughts about Rob's insides being splashed around out there. But I also know if it helps one person survive, that will be fantastic. Rob loves being in the public eye. However, I don't think this is what he has in mind.

Dr. B draws diagrams of his work. "The good news is that all the cancer is out, and it has not spread to nearby organs. We cheer. He tells us there were many more lymph nodes impacted than expected. "That's what took so much time in surgery stage one. With lymph nodes involved, it is likely cells will be in the bloodstream. This is where chemo comes in, to wipe out those cells." He pauses, looks us dead in the eyes and, choosing his words carefully, says, "I want you to know this is an aggressive cancer. When young people get it, it's bad. It most likely will come back. We must watch carefully."

My emotions surge then plummet into hell as I listen. The editors in my mind promptly slam the door on the last bit of news about the cancer coming back. Those doors never open again. My optimism steps in and stands guard.

CHAPTER 10

Intensive Care

May 29, 2003 St. John's Hospital. Santa Monica, California

EIGHT OF US PILE into the Intensive Care recovery room ignoring the signs that say, "No More Than Two Visitors." Rob is resting there, barely awake, groggy from the anesthetic. With tubes coming out of everywhere, he opens his eyes just a crack. In a voice scarcely there, he says, "I'm alive." He manages a weak smile.

Angel's sister says, "Rob, you're a survivor."

Without missing a beat, his inner comedian emerges. "I'm a Survivor? Where's my million dollars?"

We laugh and some tension falls away. But the heart monitor next to his bed is emitting disturbing high-speed beeps, an indication his heart is racing dangerously fast. Angel's relatives, crowded into the small space, bump into each other, not sure what to do.

I take charge. "Here's what we can do for Rob. We're going to act as a team, and together we're going to send healing energy to him. Rob, your job is to receive it, to let it in." I get a few glances of skepticism, but most everyone knows I dabble in the healing arts, and they are willing to try anything that might help, even this. They all listen carefully as I explain.

"Nurses use this in hospitals everywhere. Have you heard of Healing Touch? It's like that, but we're not going to touch him. Let's spread out evenly and circle his bed. Watch out so you don't trip on the tubes. Now, hold your hands out in front of you and over him like this. About ten inches above his body, palms down." I demonstrate, and my voice softens. "Take a deep breath, let it out, relax, and close your eyes. Quietly and simply send him love, from your heart, through your hands, and into his body. Keep focused on sending love. If your mind drifts off, just bring it back to sending love. And start now."

They don't fully understand the whole concept, but they all get the "send him love" part. Love is the easy thing we can all do in this complex scenario. We stand in silence, directing our energy toward Rob. What happens next is astounding.

Within one minute, Rob's heart rate plummets like Wile E. Coyote going over a cliff tied to an anvil. It drops so fast, from dangerously high to near normal, it triggers an alarm. The din breaks the group's focus. Someone, freaked out by what just happened, lets out a nervous laugh. The circle breaks, and everyone steps back as the ICU nurse rushes in to see what set off Rob's heart rate monitor. As she turns off the noise and checks the screen, I explain. "We were doing Healing Touch." Silently, with a steely expression on her face, she ushers us out to the ICU waiting room, where we take seats.

No one speaks. But everyone looks at their hands.

CHAPTER 11

Up And At 'Em

May 31, 2003   St. John's Hospital. Santa Monica, California

THE HOSPITAL WAITING AREA is welcoming with its floor to ceiling windows that splash sunshine over multiple comfy settings of couches, chairs, and coffee tables arranged thoughtfully on living room quality carpeting. Healthy plants in large ceramic pots are everywhere, and a baby grand piano sits elegantly at the far end of the room. This is where our gang of family and friends camps out each day. We support each other, take turns visiting Rob so as to not overwhelm him, and retreat back here when he says he is tired. Even though it's a short distance from here to Rob's private room, imagine our surprise when, on post-surgery day two, Rob comes shuffling slowly and cautiously into the lobby attached to his med pole.

No one notices him at first. We are huddled in a circle talking about healing when we hear a familiar voice say, "Hi." For a brief second, there is silence. Our heads swivel, and we stare in disbelief at him standing there in his blue hospital gown and slippers. We are stunned. It's like seeing a ghost.

"Rob!" We call out in unison, our eyes wide, our minds trying to grasp that he is out of bed and moving around after having his insides largely rearranged only forty-eight hours before. We rush toward him. He looks wobbly, but the physical therapist who accompanies him is there as a leaning post. The men in our group sidle up to Rob to provide additional support. Someone goes to find a wheelchair.

"I need to go back to my room. Just wanted to say 'Hi,'" Rob whispers. His face is pale, and he is sweating profusely, but he manages a smile.

As a competitive swimmer, Rob is always out to break records. Being released from the ICU and into a private room after 24 hours sets a hospital record. Getting up and around so soon is another. He is the talk of the floor.

The next day, he confesses to me that it might have been a mistake to push it by doing too much too soon. "The pain is awful, Mom."

I feel sick.

CHAPTER 12

Connections

May 30, 2003   Studio City, California

MESSAGES FROM WELL-WISHERS INUNDATE both my email and voicemail. They're mainly "What can I do to help?" and "I'm here for you." I'm not a great telephone person in the first place, so I'm feeling overwhelmed by the number of people who want to talk. For a while I try responding to everyone, thinking connecting directly with the outpouring of concern and support will help me. And to an extent it does, but I rapidly become tired of saying the same thing over and over. I feel like an echo in a canyon. And most important, I don't want to re-experience the strong emotions that surface with each telling. I'm already exhausted. It doesn't take long for me to check Caller ID when the phone rings and to scan emails, making myself available only to those I can handle, those I know will lift me up and not drag me into a deeper place.

An epiphany—I'm giving away too much of myself. I've been too concerned (irrationally) that my close friends will be disappointed if I don't call them right back with first-hand health info. I realize what it is doing to me emotionally, sapping the little reserve I have, a reserve I want to save for Rob. I have to take care of myself, let myself receive their goodwill in a way that feeds me instead of drains me.

The fix is simple and successful. I create a huge group email list. Angel does the same for her circle of contacts. When either of us is too frazzled to write, she sends my email to her group, and I do likewise with hers. We call them "Rob Updates" and send them out whenever we have news or a need to connect. Some are lengthy and thoughtful. Others are quick hits just to stay in contact and hope for loving emails in return. Messages received in response are, for the most part, thoughtful and kind. And I'm thankful I don't have to talk.

Writing Updates gives me a chance to sit quietly and reflect. It's an opportunity to be positive and look for blessings, and when I share them with my email family, I feel connected and supported.

—

Rob Update/June 4, 2003

Dear Friends,

Thanks to everyone (you know who you are) for the supportive emails and the good thoughts.

Rob ate his first food today! He said orange jello tastes better than any food he has ever had (he hasn't been able to eat for a week). He continues to amaze the doctors and everyone around him. I owe it to his positive attitude, the healing thoughts and prayers from all of you, and that he is young and strong.

Love, Ellyn

Released from parental duty for a couple days by Angel, who insists I take a break, I rent a car and drive to San Diego. Ginger and six other members of the McNally clan of cousins gather for a welcoming party. They are dear friends who have adopted me into their family by dubbing me "McWolfe." We celebrate Rob's progress, and they fuss over me as we empty a couple bottles of my favorite champagne, Veuve Clicquot. Stepping down to Two Buck Chuck, stories and laughter prevail, punctuated by tears of relief.

Good friends are exactly what I need. My tension levels are high, so getting high and getting hugs take some of the edge off, at least for the night. I drive back to LA Friday morning feeling somewhat refreshed.

While I was gone, Rob developed an infection. The antibiotics to fight it caused hallucinations and made him grouchy. As if he didn't have enough to deal with. Angel is staying with him at the hospital.

—

Rob Update /June 8, 2003

Hi Everyone,

Good news. Recent tests show that all the new internal connections are "fabulous" and not leaking. This means he is healing internally, and the newly created systems will be good to go soon. This is the second best news I've heard. "All the cancer is out" remains the top story.

He was up walking again today—we looped twice around the hospital floor, then we got on the elevator and walked to the lobby, circled the tropical fish tank and headed back to his room. His physical strength gets better with each day, his emotional strength is phenomenal, his sense of humor strong as ever.

He continues to amaze everyone in the hospital. He may be discharged as soon as this weekend if things continue to go so well. He has won round one. Round two comes with chemo, but we're staying in the present and celebrating his successes to date.

Love, Ellyn

—

Rob Update/June 10, 2003

Hi Everyone,

Emotionally, Rob has been on a downward slide the past couple days, so very sad about losing his good health and carefree lifestyle, fearing 'What if this doesn't work?', having intense pain, sick of being poked with needles, tired of being in the hospital yet reluctant to leave and lose the nursing support. He misses being home with Angel and their kitties. These are normal feelings for those who go through what he has been through. He is also coming off the morphine, which apparently takes regular emotions and intensifies them, making it all worse.

We're doing our best to listen, be encouraging, and love him. The doctors are handling the rest. Each day is a new experience filled with new hurdles to get over, so we're going one day at a time.

Those estimates of him going home by last weekend were way off.

Your good wishes, your prayers, and your cards have meant so much to Rob and to me. He cried yesterday morning as he opened a new pile of mail and said, "I never knew so many people cared about me." It all contributes to his healing.

Love, Ellyn

—

From my cheerleader-like friend, who planted an idea/ June 11, 2003

Ellyn, Are you writing about it? You already know how powerful journals are, and your story would be so helpful for others in the same situation. I look forward to hearing that you are using your writing as a healing tool for yourself and others.

xxoo Marcy

Then there is the occasional anger-inducing email. Two arrive from an acquaintance who means well, but her messages make me feel terrible. She rattles on for three pages with stories of her own suffering, and frankly, my energy levels are so low most of the time that I can't take in one shred of anyone else's problems or sad emotions. I need all my reserves to keep myself going. When I notice she is taking me down, I stop reading.

Proselytizing religion is another thorn in my side. Everyone has their own belief system, which I consider private and should not be pushed on others, even inadvertently. I do not take well to formalized religion and stick with nature as my personal source of inspiration. With an agnostic father and a fallen Missouri Synod Lutheran mother who would pause in her Sunday newspaper reading, look up and announce, "Oh, I should go to church," then pull the paper up and return to the column she was reading and not move until she needed another cup of coffee, my views were pretty well set early on. So, when this same person writes, "I am a firm believer that the Lord works in strange ways ... We must trust and hope that He will bring us and those we love through it," I become edgy. I know I constantly ask people to send prayers and am grateful when they tell me they have done so, but somehow this feels like too much and makes me balk.

The last straw for me is her heartless comment, "The stress of the situation may do Rob and Angel's relationship in." I fume and hit the Delete key. Jump in the lake is a cleaned-up version of what I am really thinking.

—

Rob Update from Angel/June 13, 2003

Hi Everyone,

Rob is home!!

It's the middle of the night in LA, and I just woke up thinking (read: worrying) about how to help Rob get the calories and good nutrition he needs for this next phase of weight and strength rebuilding. This is a direct result of my pre-sleep reading—*What to Eat When You Don't Feel Like Eating. A Guide for Cancer Patients.*

Putting weight back on when he can only eat small amounts, doesn't have an appetite, is on a fiber and residue restricted diet, and needs lots of quality nutrition is a challenge. Rob has been the family cook and now has no energy to do it, so his little meals need to be simple. If any of you have suggestions or recipes for me, please send them along!

This might sound weird, but in a way we're kind of lucky. We are discovering the preciousness of life, health, and loved ones very early in our lives ... sort of like George Bailey in *It's A Wonderful Life.*

Our bottomless thanks and love,

Angel & Rob

—

Rob update/June 27, 2003

hi everyone,

i'm back in Annisquam feeling comfortable rob is going down the right health recovery track and will be just fine getting to know his new 'bodywerks' on his own.

love, ellyn

CHAPTER 13

Bernie

July 1, 2003   Boston and Gloucester, Massachusetts

I SUCCUMB TO DEEPLY stuffed emotions at work this morning and want to be anywhere but in my windowless office, dealing with the nonsense that masquerades as business. My phone rings. It's a former Manchester-By-The-Sea neighbor (we lived there when the kids were in high school) reminding me this afternoon is Bernie G's funeral. I use this as an excuse to escape. Plus, I really want to pay my respects to Bernie, his children, and parents.

A brain tumor killed him at sixty-three, only three years after his wife Wendy died from stomach cancer.

Stomach cancer! How is it possible that both Wendy and my son, who lived less than a mile apart, both developed something as unusual as adenocarcinoma? Too much of a coincidence for me to let it pass. I search every possibility and ask Rob's oncologist about one—could the culprit have been toxic emissions from the Salem Power Plant, just across the bay? Wendy and Bernie were directly downwind. We were on the other side of Smith's Point.

"We treat each patient as an individual case. The likelihood that toxic emissions had anything to do with this is almost nil.

Look at genetics first," Dr. L informs us. "We took cells during surgery and sent them to the lab. Complex genetics mapping indicates heredity is the likely villain. It's a type of cancer that runs in descendants of Ashkenazi Jews."

Rob's biological father was the carrier of the fatal gene. Wendy's ancestors most likely came from the same line.

I drive hesitantly to the Gloucester synagogue. Something deep and fearful is pulling at me to turn and go home. I have my foot on the gas but feel as if I am riding the brakes. Funerals have frightened me since I was a small child and had to sit in a room with an open casket with my forty-two-year-old Uncle Ray lying inside looking very plastic. The lights were low, creepy music was playing, people were sad. My mom made me walk up to the body to say goodbye. I truly believed Uncle Ray would come alive, jump out and grab me (an unfortunate result of too many cartoons). Terrified, I started to cry. I remember my grandmother saying, "Oh, Ellyn is so sad. She misses him." Wrong. Next, my mom insisted I say "I'm sorry" to my aunt. I did it because my mom told me to, but I didn't understand why I had to apologize. What had I done wrong? I was too young to understand what "sorry" meant in this context, and no one bothered to explain. Death was a newcomer, and I didn't get why my cousins didn't want to play, or why my mom and her sister were crying so much.

After the funeral and reception, we went back to my aunt's house. The "big kids" (my sister, brother, and older cousin) were allowed to go to the movies, but only if they took the "little kids" (my two younger cousins and me). I don't know who had their head in a paper bag, but the movie was Frankenstein, which cemented my fear of death big time. Every night over the next year, my mother had to sit at my bedside, with the light on, until I fell asleep.

I arrive in Gloucester early. "Maybe I won't find a parking space," I say out loud. Of course, there is one right in front of my ex-husband's law office, just down the street from the temple. I wiggle my car into the space. And there he is, sitting in a chair by the window, watching and waving at me. Damn. I haven't really spoken to him since his remarriage. "Okay, a short visit might work as a distraction," I rationalize.

Into his office I go. We talk about Bernie and the last time we had seen him at Wendy's funeral, where Bernie announced he had been diagnosed with brain cancer. He considered his illness "just another amazing adventure." With typical enthusiasm he told us, "I'm starting a whole new life, one that takes me down an interesting and mysterious path. I'm excited to start the exploration and plan to emerge the champion." What a perspective. But this was perhaps the only undertaking where he did not emerge the champion.

Bob asks about Rob and wants to know how I am coping.

"His chemo will start in a few weeks. Rob is understandably scared, and I am a wreck."

I begin to feel uncomfortable, so I use Bernie's service as my excuse to exit. Now I am committed to go.

As I approach the temple, I spot Chip and his young adult son, Lee, standing outside. I've been good friends with Chip since his grinning face popped up in my kitchen window (6 feet off the ground) over twenty years ago. He jumped up and down, up and down like a Jack Russell terrier, his head appearing, then disappearing. When his foot found the water meter, he boosted himself up, smiling into my open window. "Hi, I'm your new neighbor!"

I gasped.

"That's my husband," my new friend Barbara, who was having tea with me, explained when she saw the look of alarm on my face. For Chip, using the front door was simply too conventional.

When he sees me walking toward him, his expression switches to surprise. "Ellyn! You're the last person I expected to see here." He hesitates. "Are you going to be okay? I mean, are you okay being here with all you're going through with Rob? Lee is here because he played soccer with Bernie's son, Ben. Bernie was their coach. Come with us to the reception after. I'll drive and we can pick up your car later. For the service, sit with us at the back near the door. If it gets to be too much, we'll slip out with you. I have Kleenex if you need it." Chip does have moments of normality.

To keep my emotions at bay, I try to focus on the rabbi's words and on the family stories Ben and his sister Elizabeth tell. I avoid looking at Bernie's parents sitting in the front row. Children should not precede their parents in death, no matter what age.

Though my emotions are dangerously close to the surface, I am relieved to make it through the service without a peep, or so I mistakenly think. I haven't noticed Bernie's unpretentious pine casket tucked into a niche at the front of the sanctuary, covered in a simple purple cloth bearing a gold-embroidered Star of David. A humble exit for a man who sold his business three years earlier for $200 million. His coffin rests on a waist-high bier with wheels.

The room is hauntingly still. As the pallbearers roll the casket down the center aisle toward the exit and the hearse outside, one of the wheels emits a high-pitched squeak. It repeats with each slow rotation and resounds throughout the otherwise silent chamber, squeak … squeak … squeak.

I make the mistake of looking at Chip. Instantly, laughter consumes us. Barely able to suppress it, our bodies shake as we clap our hands over our mouths, not wanting to disturb the solemnity of the occasion. The whites of our eyes turn red. Tears trickle down our cheeks. Lee looks at us, disgusted, which only makes it worse. Chip pulls out the Kleenex. "I think you need this," he whispers. That does it. I can't hold it in any longer—a loud "whoop" escapes my lips. As all eyes turn toward me, I quickly gather my belongings, dabble tissue at my eyes, cover my mouth, and slip out the door before the squeak, squeak gets any closer.

Once outside, I hear people whisper, "Poor thing, her son has cancer. This must be so hard for her." It's like fuel on a fire. Every serious thing sends me further into peals of squelched laughter. They think I'm crying, but this crazy laughter is my psyche's way of releasing the intense anxiety I've been carrying inside me.

Lee leaves with his pals, relieved to escape his dad and me. Chip finds me, alone and still sniggering, my back to the crowd. We make our escape, choking back guffaws until we're out of earshot, then we really let it rip. Skipping the cemetery and reception, we head to the local watering hole to toast Bernie, life, and the stress-relieving aspects of laughter.

CHAPTER 14

Distractions

July 2, 2003   Annisquam, Massachusetts

DISTRACTIONS HELP KEEP ME on an even keel. Daily I scour *The Gloucester Times*, our local news rag, for anything to pull me away from melancholy and into a lighter realm. If it's nature oriented, I'm interested. "Experience Seaweed!" catches my attention. A two-day workshop with a lecture, recipes, Friday night tasting, and a Saturday afternoon seaweed harvesting field trip ("Wear a swimsuit!"), sponsored by the Ecological Preservation branch of The North Shore Audubon Society. Perfect.

The North Shore Audubon Society, the largest conservation organization in New England, caters to a coastal area rife with blue blood bird watchers. Easily identifiable, they dot the landscape, often knee deep in marsh grass, always with binoculars dangling on stout chests, wearing sturdy brown shoes with matching laces tied in double knots, wide-brimmed canvas hats with under-the-chin straps held tight with a brown bead, long shirt sleeves and pants to protect against sun exposure, camera vests with multiple bulging pockets—all in muted shades of khaki, much like a female bird, to not attract attention.

They travel in flocks to pre-arranged destinations where they stand for hours. Their cameras, some with lenses larger than their heads, perch on tripods all pointing at the same pin prick on a tree limb dangling over the water. A simple turn of a feathered head or flick of a wing and the silence shatters with the mass clicking of shutters. It sounds like Oscar night on the red carpet.

I was invited by a friend to one such outing on Plum Island. I listened to them interact—

"I didn't see you at Plum Island last weekend. Too bad. You missed the Hoary Redpoll. Made a rare appearance from the Arctic. Quite spectacular! Photos are on the website, of course."

"We were in Gloucester for a wedding and got out to the old Paint Factory on Rocky Neck to see the Pink-Footed Goose everyone's talking about. Quite a trip for that fellow, all the way from Iceland. Funny what the breeze will blow in. It was a marvelous sighting."

"Did you hear that Marcus photographed a Zone-Tailed Hawk near Burrage Pond? One was also spotted off Chappaquiddick three months ago. It's almost never seen east of the Mississippi, so I wonder if this could be the same bird? What do you think?"

Audubon is largely populated by the TFB's (Trust Fund Babies), the North Shore and more casual version of the Boston Brahmin. Dedicated to preservation of nature (Audubon), the arts (Museum of Fine Arts, Symphony, etc.), the less fortunate (New England Home for Little Wanderers), education (everybody went to Harvard), and medicine (donors to major hospital wings). These wealthy families are generous and prefer their philanthropy to remain unacknowledged. Their clothing is conservative, well-tailored, and often twenty years old. Fashion? Never. Fords with no extras grace their driveways; a full-sized Oldsmobile is dangerously close to being showy. Anything flashy is considered ostentatious and, therefore, distasteful.

Friday night comes at last. I arrive for the seaweed workshop in my mid-sized Oldsmobile at the appointed time, ready to take on whatever Audubon has to offer. The room is a large, well-appointed country kitchen. Wooden tables with five comfortable chairs, all from the earlier part of the last century, fill the room. Three-and-a-half tables are filled already, a decent turnout. I slip into an open seat as close to the front as possible. My nostrils catch the scent of something delicious in the air, and my salivary glands activate.

A trim and cheerful looking woman at the front of the room arranges pots and casserole dishes alongside plates, forks, napkins and several crinkly packages of the evening's subject matter. Stapled packets of handouts sit in a stack nearby. She introduces herself as Janet and launches into the program with gusto.

Her lecture comes first, extolling the virtues of the different varieties of this little known and rarely eaten exotic. I am surprised by the high protein content (up to 25%), the antioxidants, iodine, iron, calcium, and so many more nutritional goodies in this slimy green ocean algae, and equally surprised to hear seaweed is superior to earth grown vegetables. Janet makes a point of suggesting seaweed could be a partial answer to the world hunger problem, if only people would wake up to its benefits as the Asians did thousands of years ago.

Learning about seaweed and tasting it can be two very different experiences. First on our plates is sesame laver (nori in Japan, familiarly known as the wrap for sushi), a dry mixture we sprinkle over egg noodles with a dab of butter. Delicious! Nodding heads around the room utter a surprised, "That's good!" to each other. Next, we sample Dulse Dahl, an Indian style concoction of split peas, cumin, thyme, black pepper, red chili and the seaweed dulse. I write, "Yum!" next to this recipe on my handout. This is going very well. Until we hit the kelp tastings. Patooie. Kelp is a complete taste bud reject for me. Janet offers a few more flavorful samplings, and I am back on track as a new fan of seaweed. The evening ends with a murmur of satisfaction throughout the room. We leave excited for the next day's adventure in which we will harvest our own seaweed from the long stretch of rocky shore near the Eastern Point Lighthouse in Gloucester.

I wear my swimsuit under my clothes, tuck a towel, sunscreen, and plastic bags for my harvest into my beach bag, and off I go. I arrive as others are parking. We spot Janet in the distance, sitting on a boulder at the ocean's edge, soaking in the sun. She waves as we approach.

Maneuvering over the granite rocks, Janet points out various seaweed varieties in the water and how they attach to the rocks with claw-like holdfasts. Watching this food source undulate rhythmically with the waves is mesmerizing. Fortunately, it's a calm day, and the Atlantic is receiving visitors graciously.

I have seen the other weather extreme, the Nor'easter, as it pounds the shore and terrorizes coastal communities (remember the movie, *The Perfect Storm*?). The Gloucester Fisherman's Memorial stands at the head of the harbor, honoring those claimed by the ocean. The rugged bronze fisherman braced at the wheel with the inscription, THEY THAT GO DOWN TO THE SEA IN SHIPS 1623–1923, looks out to Gloucester Harbor. And when I see the tablets inscribed with the names of over 5300 lives lost at sea, I choke up. Too many young men dead at too young an age. A tear is rolling down my cheek as I write this.

I digress, but this is exactly why I need distractions. Death is all around me. I need a break from it and time to enjoy life while I have it. And while Rob has it.

Janet gives a brief seaweed lecture, then sets us free to harvest. I step carefully into the watery garden, carefully because wet rocks are slippery like black ice in the winter. You can't see it until you're on it, and it will take you down instantly. I step gingerly onto a flat rock near a patch of Irish moss, also known as carrageen moss. (Check out the ingredients list on your ice cream carton. I'll bet you'll see carrageenan listed.) One recipe provided by Janet uses Irish moss, and here it is in abundance right in front of me. There are two variations on the recipe—one for custard, the other with only one ingredient change is for hair conditioner. I opt for the hair conditioner and set about gathering.

The water is cold, bone chilling cold, but after a few minutes when numbness sets in, it no longer matters. New Englanders let nothing as minor as temperature get in their way. After what their Pilgrim ancestors bore crossing the Atlantic, then losing nearly half their population in the first brutal winter in Massachusetts, this is nothing. I was raised in the Midwest. My ancestors are hearty immigrant stock, so I can relate. I splash along the rocks, focusing on the task at hand, never allowing myself to succumb to the elements.

I take a moment to plop on a rock and watch the others. Collectively, we look like a bunch of school kids at the beach with our plastic bags full of goodies from the sea, our teacher waiting on the shore. It's good for me to revert to a childlike state, joyful and free, splashing around, slip sliding on the rocks, getting wet and not caring.

I can't wait to get home and start cooking.

I follow the instructions carefully. The end result looks good—it has the same consistency of a slightly goopy hair conditioner. The downside is that my kitchen has a strong odor of a day at the beach near the seal rookery. I put the concoction in the 'fridge to cool and wait, hoping the odor will chill as well. Finally, off to the shower. Hair washed, I pick up the homemade conditioner and carefully apply it with visions of ultra-shiny hair and people stopping to ask for my secret. I rinse, but the stinky odors of the beach stay with me. Once dry, the smell will dissipate, I reason. Rinse again, towel dry, blow dry. I walk into the living room where my daughter is reading.

"Ewww, you smell like low tide," she says, wrinkling up her nose as she leaves the room.

I laugh as I head back to the shower. This phase of my seaweed experience is a failure. But overall, I am happy. The diversion worked, and that's what counts.

Getting away is the best distraction. If I can't get on a plane and leave physically, I leave mentally via novels. Over and over, Elin Hildebrand invites me through her pages to Nantucket, a small island paradise, thirty miles off the coast of Cape Cod and fondly known as "The Little Grey Lady of the Sea." I always thought it was so named because all the buildings in town have wooden shingles weathered to a silvery grey, but I learned it's because of the dense grey fog that rolls in quickly, consuming the town and hampering navigation. It was the sailors who named it back in the early 1800s when Nantucket was the world's foremost whaling port. I have been a regular summer visitor for nearly thirty years, so Ms. Hildebrand's words transport me non-stop to a place I know well and love.

The Jared Coffin House in the center of town was my first Nantucket lodging many years ago. It provided well-appointed and cozy 19th Century respite and the best eggs Benedict I had found anywhere. Entering the bedroom was like stepping back in time—a four-poster bed, with handmade netting draped across the top, created a space so alluring I dropped my suitcase, launched through the air, and landed face down on the quilted coverlet. Ahhh. I lay there spread eagle and sighed for what seemed like forever, imagining myself in a former life as a sea captain's wife.

Outside, the uneven brick sidewalk along the cobbled street sustained that illusion. Except for the contemporary clothing and accessories in the grey-shingled storefront windows, I could have easily bumped into Captain Ahab at the local watering hole next door, The Brotherhood of Thieves.

Today, a bike fitted with a straw basket, rented from Young's Bicycle Shop, is my preferred mode of day transportation. Driving in a car over the original cobblestoned streets shakes my bones and rattles my teeth. On a bike, the streets are impossible to navigate. Once out of town, it's free-wheeling to Miacomet, Dionis or Surfside, my favorite beaches. Each location has its own mood and attracts me depending on my own.

Dionis, sheltered by sand dunes and offering calm seas, is my quiet place to read, snooze, or simply sit on the warm sand and create little artsy sculptures out of the shells, straw, and feathers I find scattered about the area. My favorite creation is an ostrich-like bird, which I hope small children will find while beachcombing and wonder how it got there. I expect their parents to make up stories about it, like I used to do with my kids when they were small.

Miacomet, ferocious and dangerous due to crazy rip currents and pounding surf, caters to my wild side. Clumps of beach grass and daredevil surfers punctuate long stretches of desolate sand. For me, this is a no-swim beach. As I walk along the edge of the sea, the salty froth splashing fiercely over my toes and eroding the sand beneath my feet sets my imagination free to possibilities never considered before. Here I can mentally do or be anything. Nothing is out of reach. I feel both exhilarated and exhausted when I jump on my bike at the end of the day and pedal back to town.

Surfside is the middle ground. It's beach-goer friendly, offering a tidy bath house with showers, a goodie-filled snack window, and a slew of ever-vigilant lifeguards. I was there once when panicked parents realized their toddler was missing.

Within five very tense minutes, the lifeguards had 100 people out of the water looking for the child. Someone found her nearby, happily digging in the sand with a pink plastic shovel. The parents cried with relief that she was safe. The only thing that will clear the swimmers out of the water faster than a missing child is a large dorsal fin in the distance. You've never seen people move so fast when they think Jaws is circling.

Surfside is a long and beautiful stretch of soft white sand with an occasional grey shingled house partially hidden in the low dunes behind the beach, but for the most part it is pure nature unadulterated by man. The surf is just large enough to be fun, but not alarming, except for that occasional rogue wave that grabs a body surfer, tumbles her so she doesn't know which way is up, drags her along the bottom, then spits her out on shore with a swimsuit full of sand and nasty scrapes from the pebbles on her knees and elbows. Not so different from what my life feels like right now.

Nantucket's population swells from 10,000 in the winter to 50,000 during the summer. Most businesses are seasonal and high quality. Restaurants are mostly divine, atmosphere-filled, and expensive. Over the years I developed a few foodie rituals, mainly at the local inexpensive level. Breakfast is at The Downyflake. Their homemade chocolate covered donuts (for later at the beach) are an indulgent treat I adore. It was here at The Downyflake on the morning of July 17, 1999, as I slid into a red table-clothed booth with the sun streaming in through blue and white checkered curtains, that I noticed everyone in the room intensely focused on the restaurant's TV.

News about JFK, Jr's plane crash last night in the waters off Nantucket Sound is the story. It was only the day before, as the Hy-Line Ferry carried me from Hyannis to Nantucket, that I spotted the massive white tents dotting the shore at the Kennedy compound, set up for the wedding that was John and Carolyn's destination. It was eerie and sobering to have sailed through the area where their plane went down later that night, and to have seen the family homes they never reached. Too many young adults lost too soon.

Death is all around me. There is no escape. This reminds me of the ancient Mesopotamian tale about a servant who sees Death in a Bagdad marketplace. He is frightened when Death points at him, so he runs away to the town of Samarra to avoid what he presumes to be his fate in Bagdad. The servant's master approaches Death and asks why he made a threatening gesture to his servant. "That was not a threatening gesture. It was only the shock of surprise. I was astonished to see him in Bagdad, for I have an appointment with him tonight in Samarra."

There is no escape.

All my reading material comes from the Toad Hall bookstore in the Cape Ann artist's community, Rockport, a short drive from my house. Founded on Earth Day, this small granite-fronted shop gives 100% of its profits to local environmental projects. I am delighted to discover a volunteer Atlantic Ocean water clarity project that I led in my town a few years ago was sponsored by NOAA (National Oceanic and Atmospheric Administration) and funded by Toad Hall.

Creativity, volunteerism, and charity are strong on Cape Ann, and everyone pitches in to assist those who need a little extra help. One of my favorite events is the Empty Bowl Dinner, sponsored by The Open Door Food Pantry in Gloucester. Local artists make, decorate, and donate ceramic soup bowls. On the appointed evening, the public arrives in droves. Each person makes a five dollar donation at the door, selects one artsy bowl, then fills it from a selection of soups donated by the local restaurants. Bread and cookies round out the dinner shared by over one thousand people. The attendees take their bowls home as reminders of someone in need of a meal. I treasure the small white bowl I chose with the words Be Useful/Be Present/Be Hopeful/Be Grateful painted across the green rim. Its message is particularly poignant for me right now.

There are plenty distractions on Cape Ann and beyond. I keep myself busy in a variety of ways—work; dinner parties; slumber parties with my gal pals; cruising the coast in a friend's boat, anchoring, then plunging into the freezing Atlantic waters for a breath-taking swim; various tasting contests to find the best clam chowder, best turtle chocolates, best crème brûlée.

I slip into bed at night with a crossword puzzle and work it until my eyes close, and the pen in my hand slides down the page and wakes me up. As I turn the light off and settle into my pillows, my thoughts and fears about Rob are there waiting for me, vivid and terrifying. No amount of daytime distractions can keep them away. I switch the light back on.

My Grateful Journal waits on the nightstand. I read about this in a magazine as a way to shift perspective, calm down, and get to sleep. The idea is simple but powerful—I keep this notebook nearby and, when sleep is evasive, I think about then write at least three things for which I am grateful. This requires me to sit quietly in bed and shift my thoughts from panic to the good things in my life. It usually works.

May 2003   I'm grateful
- for my beautiful garden
- for good friends who care about Rob and me and provide support
- for all the prayer chains focused on Rob's healing
- for the airplane pass from Ginger that allows me to go to LA whenever I need to

July 2003   I'm grateful
- for getting away with Marilee to Maine
- for being emotionally close to Rob and Angel
- for my daughter, sister, and brother who love me
- that Rob has gained a little weight

I do mention Rob in my Grateful Journal, but it's always positive. However, on those nights when things aren't going well for him, it's more difficult to come up with something to write.

September 2003   I'm grateful
- I have a massage tomorrow
- I held a day-old duckling in my hands
- I finished tonight's crossword puzzle

When death is hovering too close, and I'm consumed with dread, there are no positive thoughts. I am grateful for nothing. The world is black. I try to think but can't even do that. My head droops, tears form in my eyes as I stare at my blanket. It's blue, a color I love. And there it is—the only thing for which I am grateful.

February 2004   I am grateful

- for the color blue
- for the color blue
- for the color blue

CHAPTER 15

Long Distance

July 2, 2003   Annisquam, Massachusetts

I TRY TO SHORTEN the distance between LA and Gloucester by calling Rob every day. After a couple weeks of this he gently tells me, "Mom, there's really not enough going on in a twenty-four-hour period to merit daily phone contact. Once a week will be just fine. If there's any news, you will be the first to know."

July 3, 2003   Annisquam, Massachusetts

THE PHONE RINGS. IT's Rob. "I went to see Dr. B for a follow-up yesterday afternoon. He handed me an envelope full of 8x10's. He was excited and said, 'I thought you might like to have these.'" Mom, they were photos of my insides during the operation. It was awful. They were gross, and I felt sick seeing them. Same for Angel. You can see them, but I don't think you should." Rob continues to fill me in about his latest post-surgery appointment.

"When I told him I was eating bites of steak, pizza, and all sorts of solid stuff, he told me I was 'way ahead of schedule' and 'healing remarkably well.' I told him about Rich and Jaci's wedding in Oregon in a couple weeks, and that I'm bummed we can't go because I'm still healing. He told me, 'Go!' So, we're going! We called Rich and Jaci, but we're going to surprise everyone else."

I hang up the phone with hope in my heart that he really is on the mend, encouraged that he is well enough to travel and be there for his best friend. It might be helpful to have the attention shifted away from him and onto someone else for a while.

I've been so sad and worried about him. Even though he's eating, the reality is he eats only tiny amounts. He has no stomach, and his weight continues to drop. Emotionally I'm at the bottom, filled with fear, living day-by-day, feeling helpless and depressed while three thousand miles away.

I get off the phone and make myself walk to Lighthouse Beach. The past eight days of rain and sixty-degree temperatures have flooded the streets and kept me inside and restless. But today it's sunny and almost ninety. My mood brightens. Shoes in hand, I stroll into the Atlantic and slowly walk the length of the beach, kicking my feet so the water foams and splashes, soaking my shorts with chilly saltwater. I'm okay as long as I stay at ankle depth, but beyond that my feet go numb from the cold. If the Atlantic ever warms up, and some summers it never does, it won't be until August.

This weekend my worry about Rob, my lack of sleep, and my general loneliness loom large, and I am at risk of slipping into depression. Getting myself out the door and being active is difficult when I'm in a funk. So, I force myself to go into town where I lose myself in the crowds and crazy activities at the St. Peter's Fiesta, the annual blessing of the Gloucester Fishing Fleet.

The street party kicks off with a parade through the red, white and green decorated streets of the Italian and Portuguese neighborhoods, featuring a life-sized statue of the fisherman's patron saint, St. Peter, draped in flowers and carried on the broad shoulders of eight local fishermen. Bands and floats make their way through the cheering throngs. The procession stops at Pavilion Beach, where the statue is ensconced on a platform to watch over the fleet and the wild party that goes on deep into the night. The energy of the people and the fiesta activities lift my spirits. I wish Rob could be here and have his spirits lifted too.

The Seine Boat Races open the next day's activities. Ten rowers, a helmsman, and a coxswain take their places in large wooden boats that look like something out of a Moby Dick whale hunt. At the gun, ten vessels surge forward from the watery start line. The bulging muscled arms of the rowers move as a single unit, each man pulling hard at his oar with long, smooth strokes as they rush forward along the grueling one-mile course through the harbor. The winners become the day's heros.

The masses, with me squeezed amongst them, gather for the Greasy Pole Contest, a crazy thing to watch. A forty-five-foot telephone pole, attached to a platform on a pier, extends horizontally out about twenty feet above the water. A red flag attached to a stick flutters at the end of the pole. Then the whole thing gets slathered with a thick coating of gooey black grease. Hung-over macho men gather on the platform. Each takes a turn trying to run the length of the pole to capture the flag. The fun part is watching the grease do its job of taking them down, like in the cartoons where a character's feet and legs spin in circles a hundred miles an hour, running, but going nowhere. While on the greasy pole, competitors appendages flail, their mouths and eyes open wide in surprise as they lose their balance, heave over the side, and splash into the chilly harbor water. Those are the lucky ones. Other guys damage their manhood as they land hard on the pole with legs splayed. They remain paralyzed there for a few seconds while the pain registers, then they slowly roll to the side and fall into the water, clutching their crotches, eyes rolled back in their heads, mouthing a sickening "Oooohhh", which gets drowned out by the roar of the crowd. I'm sure they don't notice the chill when they hit the water.

I want Rob to be well enough to lose himself in a crowd, to laugh at the crazy antics of the people around him, to be Rob again.

CHAPTER 16

Plummet

—

Rob Update (from Angel)/July 14, 2003   Two Steps Forward, One Step Back

Hi Everyone,

What a great time! We were so happy to be at Rich and Jaci's wedding. After the difficult weeks we've gone through, it was soothing to be saturated in their love, see all their friendly faces, and hear such kind sentiments!

Rob was exhausted and unable to take part in most of the wedding events, but our friends rallied and brought some of the festivities to us at our little cabin in the woods. Rich was especially touched that his best friend was there to share this major step in his life.

That was the two steps forward.

Rob was admitted to the hospital again this afternoon because his feeding tube brewed up an infection. The tube was attached to his intestines and protruded from his abdomen about seven inches. It hadn't been used since he left the hospital, but they left it in just in case his nutrition levels dropped. The doctor removed it.

The good news is—now that it's taken care of, and since Rob is such a "straight A" patient, we'll probably have an easier go of exercising and packing those lost pounds back on.

Love, Angel & Rob

This note from Angel lifts me with the news they made it to the wedding but upsets me with the unnaturalness of a tube sticking out of Rob's body, one that is horribly infected and causing him pain. The torture he is going through is endless, yet he keeps pushing forward, desperate to be normal again.

—

Rob Update (from Angel)/July 18, 2003

Hi Everyone,

Rob was released from the hospital Thursday. We went straight to his first oncology appointment with Dr. L at USC Norris Cancer Center. It was sobering. With as much as we've been through, Dr. L made us realize the real fight starts now.

USC Norris does genetic mapping on tumors to determine which chemotherapy drugs to use. Rob's cancer is aggressive and got to his lymph nodes, so there is a high chance the cancer will come back and will be VERY difficult to treat. We have to beat it now.

Unfortunately, standard chemo doesn't work for gastric cancers, so we'll have to try experimental drugs. This will be a very tough fight, and Rob will be very sick because the chemicals are super toxic.

Treatment will be once a week for six months, then radiation once a day. I'll take him after work, but we may need some volunteers to help him get to appointments.

On another front, we are getting medical bills. Healthcare costs are astronomical!! Luckily, we have an excellent insurance plan. We were worried because Dr. L is not in our regular medical group. He said he'd recommend other doctors if insurance won't cover him. Here's why we love this guy—he's willing to coach these other doctors and have them call him if they need help.

I just learned our annual out-of-pocket maximum is $5,000. Whew!!! No matter what, that's the most we'll have to spend in a given year. Insurance will pay the rest. Knowing this, we'll stay with Dr. L. He's quite a guy, interested only in the best for Rob.

Let me take a moment to say thank you to companies like mine that recognize domestic partner relationships. Without these medical benefits, we'd go bankrupt!

We are trying very hard to stay positive, but I must admit sometimes this gets to us. This is very scary. He's painfully thin, and he's got to gain weight, or he won't make it through chemo.

Love and hope, A & R

Like the rest of the family, I had become a little cocky about Rob's stellar healing. I assumed this same level of improvement would continue right through to full recovery. Oh, how this information plummets me back to earth, smacks me back to reality. I'm scared to my very core. My facade of positivity falls off and breaks wide open, exposing the raw fear and doubt I have worked so hard to cover up.

With this news, I become quiet and face the hideous possibility of Rob's death. As I write the word "death," my eyelids slowly close, my gut tightens, and my nerves vibrate wildly throughout my body as if my arm has been hacked off and is lying on the ground next to me. My brain begins to black out as my soul screams, "NO!"

CHAPTER 17

Survival at Work

August 4, 2003   Boston, Massachusetts

WORKING IN HUMAN RESOURCES (HR) is a blessing. My colleagues are naturally and professionally sensitive. They perceive my mood and ask about Rob when appropriate, check in to see if I am holding up okay, and respect those times when I need personal space. Thoughtful cards and notes, "Just wanted you to know I'm thinking of you today," show up on my desk regularly.

Back in May our HR Vice President called me as soon as she heard about Rob. "Take as much time off as you need, and don't you worry about it. Your job is safe. Just take care of yourself and your son." This simple statement has taken a huge load of concern off my shoulders.

Jerry, the HR guy for our department, stops by my office at least once a week. "Oh, hi Ellyn. I was in the neighborhood (my office is not on the way to anywhere) and thought I'd drop in. You know I'm usually at my desk, and if you want to stop in to talk or just escape for a while, please do."

Associates across the company in offices from Boston to Colorado let me know they are rooting for Rob and for me. Co-workers step in to take work off my desk and handle my requests for Family and Medical Leave Act and vacation time. Because of them the usual bureaucracy hassle doesn't exist for me. Thank goodness, because I'm overwhelmed, and filling out endless forms might push me over the edge.

My office is my daytime home. I never use the overhead fluorescent lights. Instead, accent lighting around the room throws off an inviting glow which invites colleagues to stop in. "Ooh, it feels so comfy in here!" they always say. Computer monitor, In/Out boxes, a Tiffany-style lamp with soft incandescent bulbs, and family photos sit on my huge cherry desk. Piles of papers—projects, presentations, and new programs in various stages of completion—litter the surface. My upper right drawer is a pharmacy—makeup, hairbrush, emergency pair of pantyhose, nail polish to fix chips, Hershey's kisses, and an industrial-sized bottle of Tums. Mostly I maintain a professional exterior, but my insides don't fare as well.

Coming to HR usually makes employees nervous. "Am I going to be fired?"

"No, if you were going to be fired, you'd be in Jerry's office."

I have playthings for those who are jumpy about sitting across from me, a distraction while we talk about the issue at hand. I keep a basket of small toys, feathers and rubber squeeze toys shaped like penguins, baseballs, and light bulbs within reach of their chair. The guys inevitably pick up the balls and toss them from hand to hand, the women stroke their fingers and the underside of their chin with the feathers, and, no kidding, an employee who has an idea to run by me usually picks up the light bulb and holds it over his head. From a psychological perspective, it's fascinating to watch.

Framed landscapes in bold sunny colors adorn my walls and help me pretend I have a real view to the outside. The powers that be decided last year it was a good idea to relocate all five hundred HR employees, formerly scattered across multiple floors and buildings, to a single space on a windowless floor. What a bad idea for those of us who have brains that run on solar power. My former office was seventeen stories high with a gorgeous view of the Charles River, from Harvard in Cambridge down to the Chelsea Creek oil tanks near Boston Harbor. It was relaxing and restorative to stop work for a few minutes and gaze at the sailboats on the Charles, or watch the sun hitting the rooftop gardens across the street. I have not adjusted to the lack of sunlight nor the annoying fluorescent lights.

I live one hour north of Boston and avoid the legendary aggressive drivers and The Big Dig traffic detours by taking the train. On the station platform, commuters always stand in the same spot as they wait for the train, usually reading the *Boston Globe*, their briefcases resting on the concrete by their feet. I love to shake things up occasionally, so I arrive early, place myself in someone else's spot and wait. More than once, commuters walking on automatic pilot have crashed right into me. Expecting their "spot" to be empty, they don't see me. "Oh," is all they say, usually in a deprecating tone, as they squeeze up as close as possible to where I'm standing. I'm intrigued by human behavior.

Like the others, I climb the three metal stairs up into the same purple Mass Bay Transportation Authority car. I thank the conductor in his black brass-buttoned uniform as he takes my arm lest I miss the first giant step and disappear into the clouds of stinky, oily steam billowing out from under the train. I make a beeline for "my seat," three rows from the door, right side, window seat. A group of lively train friends park themselves in the first two rows at the front of the car. Every Monday, they pass a box of Dunkin' Donuts around to everyone and bring coffee for the conductor. I look forward to this ritual, which lightens the early morning blues that come with starting a new workweek at a very early hour. We don't let passengers in the other cars know about this. It's our delicious secret.

Because I'm the work/life guru in my company, helping employees find solutions that bring more balance between their work and their overly busy personal lives, I want to see what a flexible work arrangement (FWA) is like in practice. Honestly, it's my lengthy one hour and fifteen-minute commute each way, five days a week that triggers it. I ask for and get a FWA— four ten-hour days with every Friday off. Plus, the awesome gift of working two of my daily hours on the train. Heaven!

FWA is one program I promote throughout the company, so I make myself the role model. Not everyone is on board with my schedule. Some employees are outright jealous, but it's my job to make sure they become enlightened. Not an easy task to cut through jealousy. The reality is I get more accomplished between Gloucester Station and downtown Boston than I do sitting in my office with all its distractions. Working, while rhythmically chugging along the rails, is also a safeguard. It keeps me from gazing out the window and letting my thoughts run wild to the nightmare in Rob's life and in the lives of those who love him.

Roy, the rotund conductor for our car, collects tickets and pretends to punch them, but really doesn't. Turns out he is annoyed at his boss for changing his schedule, and this is his revenge. "I don't get mad. I get even," is his motto. I later discover it's only the women who get the no-punch punch. Roy's manager must be a male.

It always takes me a while to settle into work mode in the morning and again after lunch. I go to the kitchen for a cup of tea, stop and talk briefly with whomever looks like they aren't busy, visit the people who are known sources of chocolate, and organize my drawers. When I finally focus on my work, which I love, the world stops around me. Occasionally I look up and find Susan standing patiently in front of my desk.

"Oh! I didn't see you. How long have you been there?" I ask.

"About two minutes," she replies with a hint of a smile.

"Really? Why didn't you say something?"

"I did. You were in one of your work trances. I was waiting until you came back. It usually takes you a couple minutes to notice I'm here." She smiles.

This intense focus helps my day pass quickly and productively. Hours fly by with me so wrapped up in my work that nothing else can break through, not Susan, not even my shattered emotions.

CHAPTER 18

Illness and Healing

September 9, 2003   USC Norris Hospital. Los Angeles,
California

WHAT A SWEETHEART. ROB has arranged for his Auntie Cindi, my former sister-in-law, to come to LA from Los Gatos to play with me and help out. She is a burst of energy with a dash of fun, lightening the mood all around with her happy vibes. She is also generous, arranging and paying for a cleaning service for Rob and Angel, buying a pair of gorgeous brown suede boots for Angel, picking up the tab for our shared room, dinner and some very nice champagne.

Cindi and I are in an examination room with Rob at USC Norris, a comprehensive cancer center. Angel is at work, so we step in to help with medical appointments. Since losing his stomach, it's been a huge challenge for Rob to get the calories and nutrition he needs. He eats a few bites and can't swallow anymore even though he wants to. He's full. There is no place any longer for even one more bite. Six more pounds have fallen off his once athletic frame, and he still has infectious complications from the nasty fistula that developed from his feeding tube.

USC Norris is where Dr. L, Rob's oncologist and chemo guy, hangs his hat. Cindi and I meet him today for the first time. I am drawn to him immediately. Imagine the wild brilliance of Gene Wilder's Dr. Frankenstein with shoulder-length, wavy blond hair and huge blue eyes that zero in on Rob with 120 percent focus. Combine that with the forward-projecting posture of Groucho Marx, whose body can't move forward fast enough to catch up with his thoughts. He moves like a bullet shot out of a .45, causing his flaxen locks to flow out straight behind him. Now mix in Steve Martin's handsome face, effervescence, and zany humor, and you have Dr. L.

He whooshes into the room and screeches to a halt when he spots me, his hair slamming against his neck. He exclaims, he never talks, he only exclaims, "Oh, another blonde!" (Rob is blonde.) Then he sees Cindi, "And another one!" We all laugh.

His examination of Rob is intense and serious. "Dehydrated. A few other problems. We'll fix those. A few days here and we'll have you back on the streets rockin' and rollin' in no time, Rob." His hand is on Rob's shoulder as he discusses treatment and hospital admission details. There is a two-second pause as he takes in a sharp breath, eyes closed, scanning his brain for "What else?" His sapphire eyes snap open. He flashes a brilliant smile through the room and whooshes out, his streaming lab coat nearly closing in the gray steel door.

Dr. L's positive energy is infectious. It follows him throughout the center, creating a happy buzz wherever he goes. Rob is smiling and feels energized and positive, forgetting his illness for a while. What a difference a fantastic bedside manner makes to patients in dire circumstances.

We get Rob settled into his room and keep him company, trying to maintain the uplifting mood. It works for a while, then Rob drops off into what we hope is a healing sleep.

Tonight, I'm back to Boston on the Red Eye. As I wait at LAX for a standby seat, my thoughts are crazy. I just left my son in the hospital. He is not doing well, and I'm about to be three thousand miles away. The flight attendant calls my name. A first class seat is available, which means more comfort on this miserable all night flight and a glass of champagne to dull my thoughts.

Twenty minutes is about the maximum amount of time I can sleep on a plane. It's not really sleep, just temporarily drifting away from awareness. I envy those who switch off their overhead lights, pull a blanket up to their chins and, boom, the next thing they know the sun is rising in Boston. I read the *American Way* magazine, finish the crossword puzzle, try to focus on my novel, but end up reading the same page over and over and not comprehending anything.

Rob is consuming my mind. Now that I'm flying away from LA, I'm painfully aware of what a difficult time I had seeing my son so very thin, colorless, lifeless. Hair gone from chemo treatments, Auschwitz comes to mind. This is hard to write, but there were a couple times during this visit I let myself fear the ultimate worst—he might die.

This triggers a need in me to be with Rob full time and close by, so I'm actively involved in his daily nurturing. I want to make this happen. If I could move into their guest bedroom, that would be perfect. I'll talk with them to see if it's okay. But if I'll be a burden, I won't do it. I hope they say yes. Being there for my son feels so right. Spending the winter in LA and getting out of the Boston freeze and into flowers and sunshine will be a bonus. But he's my main focus.

CHAPTER 19

Alternative Healing

November 2, 2003   Boston, Massachusetts

I'M CONSUMED WITH WORRY about Rob. The photo Angel sent shows him less skeletal, but still very ill. He tries so hard to act normal, but he feels like garbage. Even the actor in him can't muster that brilliant smile we all know so well. He doesn't express it, but I can feel his panic. My own panic thrashes around deep inside me like the Looney Toons Tasmanian devil. The dark circles under my tired eyes and my drooping posture that I try to correct but can't, belie any confidence I try to project. I'm looking for help beyond my therapist who provides me with an outlet for expressing my fears, but I need more. I need to be with those who "get it," who are in it deeply, the same as I am.

Massachusetts General Hospital (Mass Gen) Cancer Center in Boston is not too far from my office. It offers a support group for friends and family of those dealing with cancer. As I approach the main door, I know the upper floors of the building I'm about to enter are filled with cancerous bodies in various stages of healing or dying. There is fear and sadness all around. I feel it deep in my gut.

I walk into the appointed room, do a quick survey of the seven others who look normal at first glance, but the heavy silence and the body language—heads in their hands, couples leaning on each other as if they can't hold themselves upright—tell me more. I find a chair at least three seats away from anyone who might make me talk. The others are sprinkled throughout the room in a similar manner almost as if this thing that brings us together may be contagious, so we keep our distance.

I settle into my seat and look toward the group leader, a thin fiftyish woman in forest green slacks and matching sweater. She arranges pamphlets on a grey hospital table, filling time until the clock hands creep forward two more minutes. At precisely 2:00 she looks up. Her eyes sweep across the faces in the room, lingering briefly on each one as she welcomes us.

As she connects with me, I force my eyes to open wide, eyebrows arching high in an attempt to look alert. My mouth, trying to smile, falls into a weak straight line. I want to project an image that I have it all together, that I am fine because, in my mind, I've been strong for the past week. But the truth is I'm not strong, and as soon as her empathetic gaze penetrates my defenses, I fall apart and cry. I can't even speak, so I shrink into my chair and listen to the others. The intensity of the pain in the room seeps into my heart and consumes me. I make it through the hour and know this is too hard right now, and I will not return.

Sometimes I can fend off feelings or fears that are too much by imagining myself surrounded in a protective white light and grounding myself, techniques I learned during my spiritual search period so many years ago. I developed my sensitivity to a level where, when I shifted my mind into a deep meditative state, sometimes I could see colors around people, auras that indicated their mental, physical or emotional states of being. In this auric energy field, which we all have surrounding our bodies, my hands could "feel" where a person's energy flow had been interrupted, suggesting something was out of balance physically, emotionally or spiritually. But I let go of all that years ago. I try to elicit the white light as I leave the support group but can't do it.

Ten plus years ago, I had a small alternative healing practice, using a method called Mariel. Never one to follow the "rules," I included a bit of my own intuitive style, and techniques I had learned along the way. The result was a simple but powerful process designed to release blocked memories and the emotions that go with them, then "reprogram" to achieve a more positive and healthier perspective.

I discovered Mariel at a healer's annual conference in Elizabethtown, New Jersey in the 1980s. I wanted to learn as much as I could about alternative healing, and the seminars offered in its brochure appealed to me.

On the plane, I sat next to a lovely woman, a psychotherapist on her way to the same weeklong event. We talked the entire flight. Her story bewildered me. She teaches a healing process, Mary-something, "... based in Reiki ... guided by angels ... releases blocked energy ..." She talked at length about someone named Ethel, whose miracle healing led her to develop this alternative healing modality.

Ethel had been on her way to the Mayo Clinic for cancer treatment. Her plane flew threw a thunderstorm and a lightning bolt struck outside her window. In the flash of light, Ethel saw an angel who told her she was cured. When she got to the

Mayo Clinic, the doctors looked at the x-rays she brought and were confused because the tumor that was so clearly present on the film was now gone from her body.

Hmmm. My inner skeptic tapped me on the shoulder and whispered in my ear, "Oh yeah, like a bolt of lightning and angels are going to cure cancer. Science fiction. Let it go." But the funkier part of me was fascinated and did its best to kick out the skeptic. I was, after all, on my way to a gathering of alternative practitioners.

As I waited in the lobby for my accommodations to be ready, I wondered what my roommate would be like. Will she be weird? Friendly? An exotic healer? I overheard snippets of conversations as people passed by and distinctly heard the word "Mariel" multiple times. I made a mental note.

Diane from Maryland met me in the bare bones college dorm room that would be ours for the week. I knew right away she would be a friend. Bright, funny, engaging, down to earth, yet somehow ethereal. She told me she was an accountant and a massage therapist. "Oh, and I practice Mariel."

"What's with all the Mariel?" I told her about the woman on the plane.

"Oh, that's Marcia. She and Ethel Lombardi teach together. Ethel is a Reiki Master who founded the healing practice she calls Mariel. She will be here at the conference, that's why there are so many people talking about it. They're excited to see her."

The following morning, I made my way to the cafeteria for breakfast. This was a no frills venue. The frills were what we were here to learn. The huge room was filled with adults of all ages and dress from full makeup and designer outfits, to tie-dye tees and jeans with feathers attached to long sixties-style hair. All were packed into row after row of the Oliver Twist-like dining hall and were talking with great enthusiasm as if they were old friends reconnecting.

I spotted Marcia and made my way over to say hi. She was sitting with a woman I can only describe as a cross between a Midwestern grandmother and a full-sized leprechaun—pleasingly plump with permed red hair and sparkly eyes that looked right into your soul, and rosy lipstick on a mouth that smiled warmly at me. Something in her reminded me of my mom. We exchanged a brief "Hello," and I moved on to join the others in the breakfast line.

Classes began. During the day, I absorbed lectures, demonstrations, and activities on various aspects of the healing arts. After dinner, Diane and I walked across campus to an evening presentation. It was July. The intense humidity and heat lingered into the night. Dressed in a tank top and shorts, I entered a classroom that could turn a glass of water to ice in seconds. I didn't have time to run back to change clothes, so I thought I'd wait to see if anyone came in with an extra sweater. No luck, until a woman carrying a jacket walked in at the last minute and settled into a chair across the room. I jumped up and, as I crossed the room, I noticed she was the woman sitting with Marcia at breakfast. "Hi," I said. "If you're not using your jacket, can I borrow it?"

"Are you cold, honey?" she asked.

"I'm freezing!"

"Well, let's see what we can do about that. Just turn around for a minute."

Confused, but hoping she would offer her wrap, I did what she said. I heard her briefly rub her hands together. Then she placed them gently on my lower back. "Now just take this in," she said.

A rush of intense heat moved up my spine, across my shoulders, into my head and arms and down into my legs and feet. In no less than thirty seconds, I was hot and began to sweat. It was as if I were back outside in the 95-degree heat. What the ...? I wondered to myself, awestruck. What just happened? Who is this woman?

"How was that? Are you warm now, honey?" she asked sweetly.

"Yes," I blabbered. "What ..."

"Oh, the class is starting. You better get back to your seat now." And with that, I was dismissed.

Still hot, I plopped down next to Diane. "Did you see that? I can't believe ..."

"That's Ethel Lombardi," Diane said, smiling.

I knew then why I had been drawn to this conference.

***

Louise Hay, inspirational teacher and author of *Heal Your Life*, was the first to get my attention on alternative healing. I found it to be unsettling at first. What did it mean, my emotions can affect my health? But as I read more and studied stress management with Dr. Herbert Benson, a prominent cardiologist who founded the Mind Body Medical Institute at Harvard Medical School (now called the Benson Henry Institute for Mind/Body Medicine at Mass General Hospital) in Boston, I began to take the time to stop and notice my own body and how it reacts to stress, fear, and even joy. It became clear there is something to this.

Now I can't help but wonder if there was something that happened to Rob that he was not able to stomach, and that's where his cancer developed. This triggers a flashback to 1991, Annapolis, Maryland. I was in a Super Shuttle transport from the Baltimore-Washington airport to my hotel, going to visit my daughter at St. John's College. Eight doctors who specialized in oncology were on their way to a medical conference at the same hotel. I'm not shy about talking with people, always curious about where they come from, where they are going, and why. After we chatted a bit, I asked the group a question I hoped they could answer.

"I'm curious to know if there is any truth in what I've read about a correlation between strong unexpressed emotions and some diseases? If so, can we go so far as to suggest there is a relationship between the kinds of emotions people hold inside and the location of the diseases in their bodies? For example, is there any connection between women who are in non-nurtur-ing relationships—or perhaps they don't nurture themselves—and breast cancer? Or those who have intense worry, even fear about their children—do they tend toward uterine cancers? It sounds bizarre. I'm not expressing this very well. Do you know what I'm talking about?" I held my breath, nervous they would see me as a crackpot.

They all nodded together as if operating from one brain. One doctor spoke out immediately. "It sounds like you are re-ferring to links between psychosocial and behavioral factors and certain cancers. Yes, there has been some research on this, and in a nutshell, there is a likely correlation between certain behaviors, certain coping styles, and the development of cancer. But research is still in the early stages.

"Behavioral oncologists are looking at these cancer prone behavior patterns. They call them Type C, Cancer prone personalities. This personality type is unable to deal with stressful life changes. They suppress their emotions and tend toward depressive symptoms. One typical coping strategy is to defer their own needs and focus on the needs of others. I'm going to a seminar on that very topic tomorrow afternoon at the conference." The rest of the shuttle trip was a high-level exchange of related ideas among these icons of healing. I listened, in awe.

My inner skeptic, always lurking nearby in the shadows, arose occasionally and debunked Mariel and all alternative healing as rubbish. So, the shuttle encounter reinforced my beliefs, yet I only shared this conversation with my group of healer-friends. My other friends, family, and acquaintances who sided with my inner skeptic, had no idea I occasionally played in an alternative field. I was a bit of a split personality. One half was influenced by my conservative Midwestern mother who always fretted about what the neighbors would think. The non-compliant half walked the road less traveled.

Two years later, I left my Mariel practice and most of my alternative life behind to go back to college. I needed to feed my brain and gather a few academic letters to put after my name to increase my job search credibility. I was forty-five and got into Harvard where I earned a bachelor's degree in psychology. Encouraged by a professor/mentor, I kept going and emerged with a master's degree in Psychology and Organizational Behavior from the Harvard Graduate School of Education. Wow, was this really me, the little girl who grew up believing she was stupid?

I became a counselor for a few years, a job I loved, but another company bought us and replaced our entire workforce with their own employees. I took a leap away from one-on-one guidance and ventured into the corporate banking world, otherwise known as the Tums Years. This is where I have been for the past three years.

Even though I love what I do, massive work overload due to an understaffed HR department, unrealistic deadlines, and constant harassment from my extremely unpleasant manager, all mix together and clobber me with high levels of stress.

Plus, my mom's Alzheimer's advanced to the point where she was unable to live alone safely, but she refused to move to the assisted living facility my sister and I found for her. My brother didn't understand her dementia levels and guilted us for trying to "put her away." She fell, was admitted to the hospital, and because of her advanced confusion, was moved into the assisted living facility. My brother pulled her out, moved her into his home, and now finally understands the reasons behind our actions and moved her into an assisted living facility near his home. I'm responsible for managing her finances.

Take that toxic corporate mix, include the stress around my mother's Alzheimer's, and add them to my panic about my son in the battle for his life, and I am overwhelmed—at work, at home, and at night when ghastly sleep-depriving nightmares interrupt my sleep. I'm not coping well, can't even settle down enough to practice the stress management techniques I know so well and teach to others. I try to stuff my emotions, keep up a professional corporate appearance, and act as if everything is just fine. I'm aware I'm in that cancer-causing Type C behavior pattern discussed by the oncologists on the airport shuttle so many years ago.

CHAPTER 20

Sick With Worry

November 10, 2003   Gloucester, Massachusetts

SHIVERING IN A SLEEVELESS paper gown, I lie on the examining table, feet in stirrups, knees aimed toward the ceiling, vulnerable. Seems I'm having some post-menopausal bleeding, which I would normally ignore because it's fairly common, but Rob's cancer has made this a red flag priority.

"It happened twice—first for two days at the beginning of the month, then for four days last week," I explain to Dr. J.

"Lower back pain? Yeah, around this area." I gesture toward the small of my back. "Sort of a dull ache that I notice mostly at night when I slow down."

"We'll do a quick pap and see what's going on," she says routinely as she gathers the dreaded ice-cold speculum and other invasive paraphernalia. My toes curl in dread.

She disappears behind the thin paper blanket that tents across my lower half. For some bizarre reason, I'm not supposed to see her between my legs. I feel as if I have to carry on a normal conversation that suggests I'm calm and disguises the fact that my body is ready to catapult to the ceiling when she inserts the speculum. In a voice a couple octaves higher, I say,

"I'm going to New York City for a four-day work conference to-morrow morning. Is this going to trigger more bleeding?"

Dr. J stops. "Yes, there will be some bleeding. We don't have to do this if you don't want to. If it interferes with your trip, we won't. Most likely it's regular post-menopausal bleeding. Nothing to worry about. But it's up to you."

Now I'm confused. She's the doc, why is she asking me? Rob flashes through my head. "Yes. Do it."

November 11, 2003   New York City

I'm in a harrowing taxi ride through the streets of New York, heading to 21, where my colleagues and I intend to use our business dinner allowances in style. My cell rings. It's Dr. J. "Call my office in the morning to make an appointment. Get yourself in here as soon as you get home so we can go over the test results."

Damn.

For the rest of the conference, I play a familiar survival game with myself—distraction. Focus elsewhere, anywhere but what's going on in my body. The seminars, hallway meetings, and sharing of business cards take on an importance beyond their normal value. I'm early for every meeting, don't miss a single word, rivet my eyes on whoever is in front of me, and seek out the presenters to discuss the cool stuff we're doing at the bank. The days fly by. But the worry-filled nights drag on 'til the wee hours.

I get outside to escape the intensity for a half-hour each day and walk a few blocks, looking in the store windows. I'm extra vigilant when I cross the street. This isn't a distraction. It's because I have to pay attention if I want to live. The day I arrived in New York City, as I crossed the street at an intersection, a Yellow Cab ran a light and actually drove right over my suitcase as I pulled it behind me, leaving a dusty tire track across its top. The driver had the audacity to roll down his window and yell at me for getting in his way. I got a little New York crazy myself as I yelled a string of four-letter words and pounded the hood of his yellow death trap with my fist before moving on in an adrenalin-induced huff. A lot of my pent-up tension got left behind in that crosswalk.

November 17, 2003   Gloucester, Massachusetts

DR. J SITS BEHIND the enormous desk that separates us. Her face is serious, posture unusually stiff. As I settle into my seat, I try to breathe normally. My eyes are wide with fear, the air charged with tension. She looks me in the eye and says the awful words, "The pap came back positive. You have endometrial cancer."

The only thing I hear after that is, "You could have knocked me over with a feather." Then a kind of lightheaded blackness consumes me, my hearing stops working, and everything in the room becomes surreal. I see her mouth is moving. What is she saying?

I pull my consciousness back to the surface and interrupt her. "Excuse me. Did you just tell me I have cancer?"

She nods and her mouth is working again, but I'm somewhere else. I catch bits of "... oncologist ... Beverly Hospital ... tomorrow." She hands me a piece of paper with a name and number and tells me to call Dr. S today.

November 18, 2003   Beverly Hospital. Beverly, Massachusetts

I'M NOT IN DR. S's office long. After hearing my son is dying of cancer, she says, "You need more than what we can give you here," and sets up a December 1 appointment for me with the big guns at Mass Gen Hospital Cancer Unit in Boston.

I walk to my car somewhat dazed, slide in, and sit quietly for a few minutes to process all that is going on. Then I head down the 95 for my twice a month face-to-face with my nasty manager. Thinking about the toxic cells silently growing inside me, Rob's struggle to survive, and the unpleasant meeting ahead overwhelm my mind. It's raining, but traffic is moving at a brisk pace. I'm holding steady at 75mph and glance to the side of the road where a truck is pulled over. A distraught driver is talking fast as a cop pulls out his ticket pad.

My eyes flick back to the road ahead and, OH NO, the Chevy Tahoe in front of me is stopped dead. My foot hits the brakes hard and nothing happens other than a dramatic fishtail because the pavement is wet. Time shifts to slow motion, but my brain does an instantaneous calculation and tells me, 'There is no way your car will stop in time. If you're lucky, your speed will drop some before you smash into his rear end, and oh, by the way, the bumper of your little Honda Accord is about a foot lower than the bumper on the Tahoe.'

Wretched car manufacturers. It's possible I will go under his rear end and ... Oh no! Am I going to be decapitated? The seconds feel like five minutes. I watch helplessly as my car slides closer and closer ... WHAM!!!

The sound of impact is deafening, and everything goes black. I'm not sure how long I am out, but when I come to there is a strange cloudy whiteness all around me, foggy, with a diffused bright light in front of me. I'm dazed. Where am I? Is this heaven? If this is heaven ... Oh no, I must be dead!

I hear a tap, tap, tap. As my head clears, I realize there is someone standing outside my window, knocking and saying, "Are you all right?"

I'm not dead.

The misty whiteness is the powder from inside my exploded air bag. It's drifting through the car creating an eerie fog. The bright light is the sun filtered through the powder and the white nylon fabric.

Oh my god, I have to get out of here! What if there's a fire? I fumble for my door handle, and the door pops open. Whoever is out there helps me out. I reach back in and grab my purse and laptop. The Samaritan guides me to the side of the road where I collapse in shock.

What happens after that is lost in the ethers. Not sure how I get to the hospital. Somehow my daughter appears at the emergency room and drives me home. My totaled car is on its way to an automobile graveyard. Kudos to my Honda, which crumpled around me and kept me unscathed as it stopped mid-hood under the Tahoe.

I think I'll take tomorrow off work.

CHAPTER 21

Thanksgiving

November 26, 2003   Los Angeles, California

T. S. ELIOT WROTE, "April is the cruelest month," but I will wager he did not consider November and December as contenders. Holidays can burn memories, both joyful and cruel, into one's psyche. I will not forget Thanksgiving 2003. This particular holiday is both a nightmare and a blessing—mother and son, each sick with cancer, but so thankful for being together.

I freeze momentarily when I see him at the LA airport with Angel. Hopefully, I recover fast enough so they don't notice my shock. Rob's frame, once so athletic, looks like an emaciated mannequin outfitted in a too large coat. His cheeks are chiseled and sunken, and dark circles lurk under his eyes. What frightens me most is the color of his skin. It's smoky, like he has been in a fire and hasn't washed his face. Like he has been cooked on the inside ... by chemo.

I hug him, not wanting to let go, but afraid of squeezing too tight lest he disintegrate into ash. Shannon is a step behind me and awkwardly tries to get close to her brother. Their difficult childhood relationship has not gotten much better. Their hug is brief and distant.

Luggage gathered, we hurry to another terminal to meet my sister and nephew who are arriving from Chicago for this family gathering. We all know, but don't say, this might be our last Thanksgiving together.

Rob's best friend and his wife are celebrating with their family in Tennessee. They offered us their beautiful hilltop home in Silver Lake bought with the proceeds from his role in the movie, *A Band of Brothers*. We ooh and aah as we walk onto the back deck and see the HOLLYWOOD sign not too far in the distance. Could be we East Coasters and Midwesterners are a little star struck.

Later that evening we all converge at the Red Lion Tavern, a gasthaus where we think it will be fun to celebrate our German heritage and dine in the style of Grandma Hoeppner, my late grandmother from Berlin. Rich, my nephew, studied German in high school and is eager to give it an authentic try.

Our waitress, round like our grandma and dressed in a traditional dirndl, has a personality which is, shall I say, the essence of Brunhild. She listens to Rich place our orders. "Yor German ist terrible!" she barks. Our mouths fall open as she lectures on, waving her pencil at Rich. "Vere dit you lern zis? It ist da lanquitch of the lower class!" We burst out laughing. "Ach!" she exclaims as she stomps away toward the kitchen. It's good to see Rob perk up and join in the revelry. Brunhild returns shortly with plates of sauerbraten, roulade, potato pancakes (the best I've ever eaten), schnitzel and a large sampler of the best of the wurst. Rob yum's as he eats a few bites from the sausage platter and sips some beer, the totality of what his body can hold. Watching him enjoy himself makes me happy.

Rob hates Thanksgiving. It began when he was three years old. As our little family was finishing a post-holiday left-over turkey dinner in the dining room, I noticed Rob's lips turning red and swelling. My mothering instincts sharpened. He began to wheeze. An alarm rose within me when I saw red bumps sprout across his face and arms. Almost immediately his breathing became strained, and his face ballooned. He tried to cry, but all that came out was a raspy inhale that nearly paralyzed me with fear and terrified him.

"Ric, something's very wrong with Rob."

"I'll get him into his snowsuit, and we'll be in the car. You call the emergency room at Newton-Wellesley." My husband grabbed Rob and moved toward the front hall coat closet. I ran to the kitchen phone.

"This sounds like an allergic reaction," the nurse told me. "Keep him as calm as possible and get him over here right away. We'll be waiting for you."

Ric and I sang "Old MacDonald Had A Farm," "The Wheels on the Bus," and other three-year-old favorites for the fifteen-minute, but it seemed like an hour, drive to the hospital. It worked. The songs distracted Rob (and me) enough to keep the panic down.

The result—he's allergic to poultry. No more normal Thanksgivings for him. From that day on, a medium rare filet mignon with stuffing (baked outside the bird) and broccoli casserole became his Turkey Day fare.

We gather at Angel's parent's house for today's feast with the rest of her family. Rob won't admit it, but I can see he is consumed with pain. He bypasses the party and wobbles directly to the bedroom where he falls into a deep sleep and only wakes up when dinner is ready, several hours later. He grimly faces his overdone steak and nibbles on mashed potatoes. Two bites and he declares himself finished. I wish Rob and Angel were at my house with my family and my cooking.

The next day we all head out for lunch and a walk around a huge pond in a Buddhist sanctuary somewhere in LA. "I'm surprised at the tranquility in the midst of the city's chaos," I say to no one in particular. One quarter of the way around the pond, Rob says, "I want to go back to the car." We are stupid and encourage him to go on, which he does because he tries so hard to keep up and be normal. After several rest stops on shady benches, he makes it back to the car, but he is pale and not steady on his feet.

"Do you have any aspirin?" he asks me.

"Sure. How many do you want?"

"Eight or ten," he says. I immobilize for a brief second and look him in the eyes. I see such sadness there and swallow hard, willing my tears to stay away. For the first time, I understand how bad his pain is.

Our last night together. Rob invites us to Vermont, the restaurant where he proposed to Angel. So much of this trip involves eating, and the irony is that Rob really can't—he has no stomach and is too sick. The owners are thrilled to see Rob and Angel walk in the front door. They shout out from across the room, "Where have you two been?" They approach, and I can see their eyes widen as they get a closer look at the emaciated Rob, but they make no remarks and hug them warmly. Later, as I slip out to the ladies' room, one of them takes me gently by the arm and asks what happened. Tears well up in their eyes as I explain.

Back at the table, an idea pops into my head. "Let's do a progressive toast! We'll go one-by-one around the table and say what we are thankful for." Everyone nods. I can see they are formulating thoughts. No one here is shy. They like the idea. It's an opportunity to verbalize what they have been wanting to say but haven't had the chance.

I begin. "A toast to the coming year which begins right now. May it be filled with love, with joy, and with very good health and healing."

"Here, here" is the response as glasses are held high.

Shannon goes next. "To this year in which I have gotten to know my brother better. And to many more years of continuing to know him."

Satisfied "Yeses!" spout from the table. My heart fills. I would love to see their relationship healed.

"To family and to this gathering and to all of us meeting and sharing a dinner together next year in Prague at Rob and Angel's wedding!" offers my sister.

"To a wedding in Prague," we call out in unison.

Now it's Rob's turn. He faces Angel and lifts his glass. "To this woman, who I want to call my wife, who is my wife in every way except on paper, who has been there for me in such incredible ways. Without her I would not have been able to make it to where I am today."

Angel responds to him, her glass meeting his. "Last night Rob and I, before we went to sleep, listed all the things we're grateful for, and the list was long. But the one thing I want to toast is cancer because it has given us the incredible gift of knowing the difference between what's important and what's not important in life and love. Without it we would have continued, caught up in our busy lives, and not known the sharp distinction between the two."

The honks from noses being blown, the staccato gasps for breath, and everyone asking, "Do you have another Kleenex?" while wiping their eyes, fills the space around our familial table.

The owners must have been watching from the shadows because at this point, they approach with ornate and colorful paper crowns from Bali, which they place on Angel's and Rob's heads with fanfare and good wishes for the future. It's the perfect ending to a perfect dinner.

CHAPTER 22

Pre-Surgery

December 1, 2003   Massachusetts General Hospital Cancer
Unit. Boston, Massachusetts

SHE CAN'T BE MORE than sixteen years old, I think, as Dr. D
walks into the room. She's a tiny thing with a pixie haircut, big
blue eyes, and a giant smile that puts me somewhat at ease.
She already knows everything about my medical history and
takes plenty of time to explain my kind of cancer and congrat-
ulates me on catching it so early. "If you have to have cancer,
this is the kind you want. It's contained in one neat little package, your uterus, and because you caught it early, it's likely it
has not spread." My shoulders come down a bit from my ears.
She describes the complete hysterectomy process and stops
frequently to answer my queries. She points to the list of questions in my hand. "You haven't asked that one," she says.

I look at her quizzically.

"I've learned to read upside down," she explains. "Some patients are reluctant to ask certain questions. I want to make
sure they all get answered." I take this as a big plus and relax
a little more. She is attentive to detail and cares about her
patients.

"How many of these do you do in a year?" I ask the one I held back, not wanting to insult the woman who will be taking a scalpel to my body, but still thinking she's newly out of medical school, and I'm her first surgery.

"Let's see. For the past eight years, I've done about two hundred per year. Endometrial cancer is my specialty. You thought I was a newbie, didn't you?"

"Uh, yeah."

"It happens all the time," she says, shrugging her shoulders and grinning. "I have four kids, ages six to twelve.

"I can schedule you next week, or if you prefer to wait until after the holidays, we can do that. But honestly, most women, when they know they have cancer cells in them, want them out as fast as possible."

"Next week works for me," I say immediately.

***

I call Rob first. "Hi Mom. What's up?"

I pause, take a deep breath, and let it out slowly so I don't sound as tense as I really am. "You might not believe this. I don't really believe it myself. It's surreal. I have cancer, Rob."

There is no sound at the other end of the phone. "Hello?" I say.

"Mom. What do you mean? You have cancer? You have CANCER?" He repeats it as if I have misspoken. "What kind of cancer? What stage is it? Are you going to be okay?" I hear him gasp for breath. He's upset.

This is the last thing I want. He needs to be calm and focus all his energy on getting strong. He's not doing well. I feel guilty about telling him my own troubles. Screw me and my health. He's all that is important, all I care about.

"When's your surgery? I'm coming. I want to be there for you."

"Oh, Rob." I pause, gathering the right words. How do you tell a child who body is failing him, not to come, not to bring the love he needs to give, and I need to get? "You know I want you here, but I have to say no. You need to take care of yourself first. The strain of flying across the country might be hard on you right now. I will be okay. Dr. D said I've caught it early, and with surgery, I should be back to normal in no time. Really.

"And one more thing. I owe you a huge bucket of thanks. If it hadn't been for your cancer, I wouldn't have paid any attention to my symptoms. I would have let them go, assuming it was all normal menopausal stuff, and I wouldn't have caught it in time. But I did, thanks to you. So, I will be fine, and when we're both feeling better, I hope you and Angel will come here. We'll have a lot to celebrate."

"But ... I want to be there to support you," he says.

"I know that. But Shannon is here, and I have a slew of friends who are planning to step in and take care of me. You know I love you and want to be with you, but this is not the time.

"I'll tell you what else. If I could make a deal with the universe to take me and heal you, I'd do it in a flash. In fact, I've already put that out there, many times. I've had a long and wonderful life. I would be happy to step out of it, if it meant you could be healthy."

At that we both cry.

It's natural to wonder where disease comes from. Is my offer to trade my life for Rob's really that powerful? I think about those oncologists with whom I shared an airport shuttle ride years ago and the conversation we had about how strong unexpressed emotions can result in illness. Here is my son with a serious cancer, and here am I worried to death (an ominous phrase) about him, and I develop uterine cancer. Is there a connection?

Sometimes yes. Sometimes no. I never want anyone to feel as if they are to blame for their illness. Sometimes "A cigar is just a cigar," as Freud said. Sometimes disease is just a matter of genetics, and sometimes it's the result of environmental influences, like living in a house built on a toxic waste dump.

CHAPTER 23

Surgery

December 11, 2003   Annisquam and Boston, Massachusetts

I OPEN MY DOG-EARED copy of *Prepare for Surgery, Heal Faster*, a gift from the author, Peggy Huddleston. Several handwritten notes fall out of the book onto the couch—notes from friends who borrowed it, thankful for the mind-body techniques that helped them get through their medical experiences with optimistic outlooks and inner calm. Rob is the last one to have read it. Little did I know I would be next.

A few of her ideas are things I've already been doing with Rob in mind. One, send positive healing affirmations out to the universe. Two, sit in meditation to quiet my mind and body. The third is something new—write a list of positive statements for the surgeon to read aloud during the procedure.

Dr. D likes this idea and makes an additional suggestion. "Bring music that makes you feel good, and I'll play it in the background as I operate." I tuck a CD of soft rock favorites into my hospital bag.

I believe a positive attitude will triumph over pain and speed my healing. But I am also anxious about feeling nauseous from the anesthesia when I wake up. I fear throwing up will strain my stitches and hurt like hell. And ever since that New Year's

Eve when I was eighteen, the thought of vomiting makes me, well, nauseous. My affirmations go like this:

Dear Dr. D,

Please say these aloud several times during my surgery.

Thanks, Ellyn

Ellyn, Following this surgery—
- You will feel comfortable.
- You will feel refreshed.
- You will heal quickly and easily.
- Your surgery went very well.
- You will heal beautifully.
- When you wake up in post-op, you will feel hungry and thirsty and be able to eat and drink comfortably.

It works. Post-surgery I'm ready for some ginger ale and a few saltines.

My room is filled with flowers and a snarky roommate who enjoys watching awful TV shows at high volume. She has no flowers, no visitors.

"I don't really have space for all these," I say to her. "Would you like some flowers for your table?" She smiles an acceptance and lightens up as she selects pink lilies and yellow roses.

I conk out and sleep soundly despite the (slightly lowered) noise.

By the next evening, I decide I'm going to do a Rob and set a new hospital record for healing. I ease myself out of bed, put on slippers and a robe, and start off on a slow shuffle around the hospital floor. At the farthest point out, I'm aware that my pain level is rising sharply, and I can't make it back to my room. Now what? I'm off the beaten track, and no one will find me here. I creep painfully around the corner and stop across from the elevators. The wall holds me up, but not for long. I'm sweating and wobbly.

The elevator doors open and there is my new boyfriend, who reacts with a surprised smile, then rushes over when he sees I'm struggling. He gets me back to my room and fusses over me. I'm thinking he's something special because we were a fairly new couple when I was diagnosed with cancer, and he did not run away when he heard the bad news. And here he is, with more flowers.

My daughter, Shannon, is a gift from the gods. She happily moves into my house with her kitty and becomes my driver, chef, and assistant who tackles all paperwork, communications, and keeps my calendar. There is nothing I have to worry about. And she makes me laugh.

We both love Dave Barry's column in the *Boston Globe Magazine*. She reads it to me on my first Sunday morning at home. His zany humor tickles me. I laugh and, as she reads on, I can't stop laughing. Tears pour down my cheeks. This guy is crazy funny. My friend Charles, a surgical nurse, told me to hold a folded towel to my belly if I have to sneeze or cough to absorb the shock. I wish I had known that also applies to laughter because I feel a sharp pain where my uterus used to be, and my laughter turns to tears.

"I think I popped some stitches!" I wail, holding my abdomen with both hands. "The pain is awful!" The cumulative tension that I've been holding inside breaks loose, and I become hysterical. Shannon grabs me and holds me until I cry myself out. I slump into her arms, grateful to take in her love.

I don't like medications and avoid them whenever possible, plus I think I'm feeling better with each day, so I take only half my prescriptions, then I skip a dose completely, and the excruciating pain comes roaring back. "You heal faster when you're not in pain," Dr. D scolds me. "Take your meds!" Lesson learned.

I'm grateful for my friends. They have organized and checked in with Shannon for direction. Kathleen gathers info from the others—when are you available? What can you do to help? She fits everyone into a two-week spreadsheet with instructions to call first to see if I'm up for their visit. How brilliant she is to do this and to make sure everyone does not show up on the same day, all bearing gifts of blueberry muffins.

Monday, Jane and Max bring lunch, dinner and cute, soft cotton pajamas speckled with sheep. I dub them, the "lambie jammies" and wear them that night. Tuesday, Mary's husband does my grocery shopping and, knowing I love movies, brings a stack of videos from their collection. Wednesday, Natalie comes with a giant bag of bagels and salmon mousse. She pulls two bottles of essential oils, bergamot and coriander, from her pack and gives me a reflexology foot rub while updating me on who is doing what to whom and why. I tell her I feel like Jesus being anointed. She is studying for the ministry and laughs at the analogy. And so it goes. My healing speeds along.

December 17, 2003   Annisquam, Massachusetts

THE LABS ARE BACK. Non-invasive endometrial cancer. Level One.

It didn't spread. I'm free and clear! I don't need chemo or radiation. This cancer is more like having the flu—one day it's there, the next day it's gone. Now it's about healing my body over the next couple months and coping with the emotional aspects of losing my female parts. Is all my estrogen gone? Will I still be feminine? Oh no, will I grow whiskers? Can I still have intercourse? Will I be able to have orgasms? These are valid concerns, but I don't dwell on them because, compared to Rob, they are ridiculously minor.

CHAPTER 24

Setback

December 22, 2003   Annisquam, Massachusetts

MY TEMPERATURE IS ELEVATED. Waves of pain pound my abdomen. Shannon cancels my visitors and calls the doc. "Stay on the ibuprofen with codeine, and I'll call in some Vicodin," Dr. D says. "Take it easy. Don't push yourself to do more than you can. If it hurts, stop."

I desperately want to go to LA for Christmas, but the reality is I don't think I can physically make it. Yesterday Shannon took me for a "let's get out of the house because I'm getting shack-nasty" ride in my new Jeep. Climbing into the passenger seat was not easy, and the New England crop of winter potholes we hit caused considerable internal distress.

The phone rings mid-afternoon. It's Rob. "I'm back in the hospital, Mom." He steadies his voice. "The cancer ... The cancer has spread. It's now in my hip bones and in my spine. And, I'm scared," he whispers. "Mom, this may be my last Christmas."

This is bad. Rob never looks on the dark side.

"I'm coming," I tell him. "I'll be there Christmas Eve."

Darkness threatens to overcome my consciousness. An explosion is set to detonate in my head. I try to fight them off but fail and blank out on what happens after that. "This may be my last Christmas" ricochets wildly throughout my mind. There are no words to describe my turmoil.

CHAPTER 25

Christmas Eve

December 24, 2003   Logan Airport. Boston, Massachusetts

ELEVEN DAYS HAVE PASSED since my surgery. I'm doing pretty well mentally, but physically I creep along like I'm ninety. Moving too fast causes pain, which is not good on Christmas Eve at the crowded Logan Airport. Terrified someone might crash into me with their carry-on or bump me as they dash to their gate, I made arrangements for a wheelchair.

Shannon walks me to the check-in counter, puts my bag on the scale, and hugs me goodbye. In a few minutes a blue chair comes wheeling around the corner powered by a cheery airline employee with a holiday scarf wrapped around his neck.

"Ms. Wolfe, your chariot awaits!" He sweeps his arm across his body as if he is Galahad who has dropped his cloak across a puddle, so I won't soil my shoes. Hanging my purse and pack on the back of the chair, he offers his arm and eases me into the chariot.

We whiz past the extra-long queues of time-anxious travelers at security. I'm amazed and hurt by the number of dirty looks aimed my way. I try to step out of myself and see from their perspective—I look fairly healthy, I'm smiling and chatting with my "driver," and sailing past those who have been waiting far too long to get through the security checkpoint. Fake, I imagine they are saying to their spouse, there's nothing wrong with her.

Merry Christmas to you, I think back at them. It makes me wonder what's it's like to be handicapped and have to deal with this on a regular basis. Rob and Shannon's elementary school created a program where the non-handicapped kids wore blindfolds or moved about in wheelchairs for a day to increase their sensitivity to those with disabilities. I wish more schools did that.

Galahad takes me to the "Disabled" lane and puts my bags on the x-ray machine belt. "I'm afraid I can't take you to the other side. You'll have to walk through on your own."

"I can do it." I make my way through my umpteenth x-ray in the past couple weeks.

As I exit, my ride is nowhere to be seen. He didn't say he couldn't go through security, but he didn't say he would. Mary, the TSA attendant, radios someone on my behalf. "It'll be thirty minutes 'til a chair is free. We're busy tonight. Sorry, hon."

I walk away slowly. Passengers in line are still staring at me. I feel it on my back. Maybe I should limp, I think. Good grief, I'm either going crazy, or I've taken too much Vicodin. Hugging the wall, I continue to the gate at a snail's pace.

"Thank you, Ginger," I whisper as my name is called from the stand-by list. I'm on!

"We have a seat for you in first class. Is that all right?" the ticket agent asks with a smile.

"Oh, that's spectacular! Thank you."

I pull a bath towel from my bag, fold it in threes, and tuck it around my middle. I fasten the seat belt over it per Charles' instructions. "You don't want that belt to push into your stitches if you hit turbulence," he told me before I left home. "And, be sure to get up and walk around every hour. You don't want deep vein thrombosis." How nice to have a friend who can scare the wits out of me while trying to protect me.

A nice-looking man, fiftyish, wearing tan slacks and a navy blazer over a golf shirt is seated next to me. He keeps glancing at my face as discreetly as he can, but I'm aware of it. Maybe the towel aroused his curiosity. I look at him and say, "Hi."

"Forgive me, but did you have surgery a couple weeks ago?" he asks.

"Yes. I did. Geez, do I look that bad?" I give him a quizzical look.

"Was it at Mass Gen? And Dr. D was your surgeon, right?"

I'm freaked out. "How do you know that?"

"I'm Dr. M, your anesthesiologist," he says.

"Oh, my gosh! I'm sorry I didn't recognize you. I was kind of out of it when we met."

"Yeah, that happens a lot. I was standing behind you, upside down to you, wearing a mask, then I conked you out. No one ever sees me. I'm the invisible guy in the operating room."

We both laugh. My belly twinges from the jiggle. Take it easy, it warns me.

I thank Dr. M for not letting me wake up in the middle of the operation. Then I pause, not wanting to be a wuss, but go ahead anyway. "I'm nervous about flying so soon after my surgery."

"I'm here if you need me," he says.

I'm so relieved. What are the chances I'd sit next to a doctor, and one who was involved in my surgery? This is a gift.

The flight attendants lavish attention on me for the next six hours, more so than anything I have ever experienced on a flight. Chocolates, champagne (which I can't drink because I took a Vicodin. "Maybe cocoa instead?") and a filet mignon that's over the moon. I even get a CD player with a folder of CDs, a shoulder rub, and they tuck a blanket around my legs so I'm cozy. It's only after I call Ginger, who spent thirty-plus years at American Airlines "slinging hash in a rocket" and who knows most of the flight attendants, that I find out why. "Well, maybe I made a little phone call," she says. Another gift.

Out the window, the landscape shifts from grey overcast, snowy, and barren to sunshine, green, and alive. I peel off my winter layers and relax a little thinking about the gentle climate in LA, the palm trees, and the gardens brimming with dazzling flowers in December. I also remember yesterday's 6.5 earthquake near Paso Robles, and my serenity shatters.

I spot Angel at the baggage claim carousel. A native Angeleno, she shrugs off the seismic activity just as she shrugs off the nightmare LA traffic. "It was two hundred and fifty miles away. And no significant damage. Nothing for us to worry about." She grabs my suitcase, tosses it into the Honda's trunk, and dives into the freeway traffic. "We'll take the 405 to the 10," she says. I love how Californians put "the" in front of freeway names and numbers. I'm in awe over how casually she weaves in and out among the Ferraris, the Range Rovers, and the rusty clunkers with bumpers attached by rope. Chatting breezily, she zig-zags us to the hospital.

Angel slides into a "Visitors" parking space and shuts down the engine. Quiet fills the car. For a few seconds we search each other's eyes and nod knowingly, then reach for the door handles.

The USC Norris Cancer Center doors slide open automatically. We step into the lobby. Angel hears me suck in my breath and takes my hand. We find Rob in a sunshiny private room reading the *LA Times*. He's propped up by several pillows and tucked under a hospital green blanket with a white sheet folded neatly over the top. He lowers the newspaper and looks up to greet me. A closely trimmed beard frames his face. "I like it, the beard," I tell him.

"I got sick of shaving. It's such a pain in the neck. It itched like crazy the first week."

We sit, chatting as if nothing is wrong—as if we met for a coffee and the news. This is nice. When someone is so sick, illness becomes a constant topic of conversation, and frankly, it's not healthy. Rob wants so desperately to feel normal, to act normal, to talk about everyday things. He's tired of people looking at him with eyes full of alarm and asking, "Are you okay?"

He wants to know about my health. "I'm doing great," I lie. He picks up on my fib. The deep circles under my eyes, my pasty complexion, and walking like I've just given birth give me away. Besides, he knows me.

"Why don't you go home and have a rest, then come back here with Angel for dinner. You can eat mine," he half laughs. "I'll let the maître d' know to set a table for three."

CHAPTER 26

Christmas Day

December 25, 2003   USC Norris Cancer Center. Los Angeles, California

ANGEL LETS ME SLEEP in and goes ahead to UC Norris for some alone time with Rob. Ric, who flew in from Seattle last night, is at the Hilton. He picks me up at ten o'clock. Egg McMuffin and coffee at McDonald's drive-thru is our breakfast, noting what a far cry it is from the apricot kolachky I used to make every Christmas morning back in the day. The carless freeway, abandoned as if there has been an alien invasion and we haven't heard about it, makes for a fast trip. "This must be what it was like when my parents lived here during the war in the 40s," Ric says as he speeds along. We walk into the hospital at ten twenty-five.

We've been divorced for so long, I barely remember what it was like to be married to him. I was nineteen the summer after my sophomore year and pregnant with Rob. He was twenty and about to return to Cambridge for his senior year at Harvard. We stuffed his tan VW Beetle with as many of our belongings as we could squeeze in and made the thousand mile trek to a new life.

Dr. Krister Stendhal, Dean of the Harvard Divinity School and the man who was going to marry us, was overly tall with rigid arthritic posture. He oozed intimidation as he looked down his nose at us sitting across from him. Plans for our wedding service at Appleton Chapel in Harvard Yard were crisp and to the point, until he asked what music we would like.

"I don't know the name of this hymn, but I love the music," I said and hummed a few bars then offered a choppy version of the words. His face melted into pure bliss. I could almost hear the music continue in his head.

"Oh yes," he said nodding, "that's a doxology sung to the tune of The Old Hundredth. That happens to be my favorite as well. A very joyful choice."

I loved the music, but little did Dr. Stendhal know that for me it signaled the end of the Sunday service, and as a child forced by my mother to attend church and Lutheran confirmation classes, it also signaled escape. Was this selection a forerunner of things to come with this marriage?

Ric and I were divorced when Rob was ten and Shannon was seven. I had been a stay-at-home mom until we split, and I'm grateful now for those early years with the kids—baking cookies, kissing hurt fingers, organizing birthday parties. Who knew then how important each of these loving acts would ultimately be?

Here we are, Ric and I, twenty-four years after our divorce. Together again, visiting our son for his last Christmas ever. How can it be that Rob was a healthy little boy wired to the max on Christmas morning such a short time ago? We are cordial. He is remarried to a younger woman, which I surmise, helps him maintain his marathon runner's physique. He seems happy, but how can I know that? He doesn't talk about his feelings, never has, just covers them up with jokes, kidding around, and a dose of alcohol. He's brilliant—got into Harvard as a sophomore right out of high school—but tortured inside by some demon unknown to anyone but him. It will be interesting to see how he handles this visit.

Rob is where I found him yesterday, tucked in bed, but today he isn't smiling. He doesn't move. Only his eyes shift slowly in our direction. His head rests back on his pillows, his arms sagging at his sides. Angel is feeding him something pink through a straw, but he's not making much headway in drawing the liquid into his mouth. Ric offers a cheery greeting and makes a light "Merry Christmas" comment to soften the surface of our fear.

"Merry Christmas. I'm ha ..." Rob starts to answer, but he falls asleep before he can finish.

Ric and I exchange glances, eyes wide. We look at Angel. "You know the cancer has spread to his spine and hips," she says. "He's in a lot of pain. The drugs help, but they do a number on him."

We pull chairs close, sit down and wait.

It's Christmas, a day to exchange gifts, but what kind of present do I get for my son who is dying? I want to have something for him, a token of love, but the last thing he needs is "stuff." When he wakes up, I greet him with, "Merry Christmas, my wonderful son. I'm so happy I'm here with you." And I touch his cheek gently. I offer my hand-written card with a slightly gooey verse I wrote filled with love, special memories, and a little humor.

Rob lifts one arm to accept it. He struggles to raise his other arm. Finally, he has the sealed envelope resting in both hands in his lap. He tries to push his finger under the flap to open it, but he can't do it. He tries again, gets his index finger under the flap, but he's too weak to tear the paper envelope open. He looks to Angel for help. She rips it open, pulls the card out, and exclaims "OH!" as a wad of hundred-dollar bills falls onto the bed.

"I didn't think a surfboard would be right." I smile. "Maybe you and Angel can use this for a little getaway when you get out of here. Go someplace that feels great and be happy to be away together." (Or use it to pay those mounting bills if, heaven forbid ... you don't get out of here.)

Ric and I slip out as Rob falls asleep again. We walk to the lobby where several decorated Christmas trees adorn the space. We move chairs, tables and couches around the tree closest to the piano, creating a cozy setting where the rest of the relatives can camp out with us and celebrate this day together. Sunlight pours in from the floor to ceiling windows and bathes us in its radiance.

The gathering begins at noon. Angel's parents, sister and her husband, her aunties and cousins pour into the lobby filled with happy energy, presents, games, and several steaming bags of Chinese takeout. Aunt Linda, a professional clown on weekends, opens a sack and pulls out a mass of red bulbous orbs. "Rudolph noses!" she exclaims as she passes them out to all of us, the two visitors at the other end of the lobby, and the desk staff. "Let the party begin!"

The next three hours fly by. Board game winners do Rocky victory dances, empty food cartons and plates litter the tables, stories get exchanged. A wheelchair, propelled by a nurse, comes slowly around the corner, and there is Rob wrapped in a robe and blanket. "Rob!" we all exclaim and rush toward him, take over the piloting of the chair, and whoosh him into the circle of fun.

He catches the energy immediately and tells a couple stories about life in the hospital that leave us in stitches. We know his bounce-back is drug-induced and likely to be short-lived, so we make the most of our time with him. Someone sits down at the piano, someone else produces a microphone, and we belt out show tunes and a few carols to mark the day.

Cousin Kerry opens her laptop to show us her new work as a videographer. Rob loves what she is doing. Heads together, they shift into their respective creative minds and get lost in an artistic discussion. Rob's eyes shine with delight. We open presents—a handsome homemade wool cap, "For the newly hairless," which Rob dons and wears for the rest of the afternoon, a black cashmere sweater for Angel, and so on until there is a large pile of crumpled wrappings on the floor.

The circles under his eyes and waning smile signal Rob's fatigue. But he tries to rally. He whispers something to the piano player, and they move together toward the ivories. Rob takes the mike, turns it on, and taps it a few times to get our attention. We gather around and applaud. "Thank you. Thank you," he says in mock Las Vegas style. "One closing song for all you wonderful fans out there. I want to thank you for coming. I love you all." His eyebrows wiggle up and down. We laugh.

Singing softly, he sidles over to the curve of the baby grand and makes a valiant effort to hop up onto the top, emulating the cabaret torch singers, but with a touch of silly. But this once awesome athlete no longer has the strength to make it and nearly falls to the ground. Ric grabs him and holds him until he is steady on his feet. The group becomes interested in invisible specks of dust on and around our chairs, trying not to register his embarrassment. Ever the actor, Rob keeps singing to the completion of the song, but we can see that the drugs that lifted him out of his extreme pain for a few hours have worn off. We applaud thunderously. Then his dad leads him to his wheelchair and escorts him back to his room.

Our group is subdued. We linger in the lobby, quieter, reacting much like we've witnessed an atrocity on the evening news. I stretch out on one of the couches and sink into a fitful sleep. I dream I am a young child standing high on a cliff, a wilderness river far below me. Several birch bark canoes paddle by. The people in the canoes spot me. They begin to throw miniscule pinecones at me, which steadily grow in size until they are enormous. I stand there helpless, unable to move, unable to defend myself. I wake in a sweat.

My festive red wool jacket feels suffocating. My belly and its stitches ache from too much activity. Slowly I walk to the ladies' room where I splash cold water on my face and neck. I dabble a damp paper towel across my chest and underarms. And I cry.

***

"Hey, what's wrong with this party? I guess you need an MC. Here I am!" Rob enters the lobby for a second act. Miraculously in just an hour-and-a-half, with the gift of powerful pharmaceuticals, he's temporarily back to his old happy self. He plies his craft well, and the room instantaneously comes alive. I trick myself into believing this is genuine joy on his part and not acting, nor drug induced. This is my last Christmas with my son, and I would like to have good memories, happy memories to carry with me.

The pizzas someone ordered arrive. There is always someone in LA who stays open on Christmas to make a buck. Four of us gather around the Scrabble board. Not only does Rob win, he snags the highest single score with "zephyr" on a Triple Word. We didn't let him win. We're all too competitive for that. The group relaxes into our holiday nest and continues comfortably for the next two hours as normal families do on special occasions, talking, laughing, being together. At seven-thirty the party draws to a close. Rob hugs me a little extra long and kisses me on the cheek. "You take care of yourself and get some rest," he says. "This was a wonderful day."

"I agree. A wonderful day, Rob. I love you."

He grabs me again in an affectionate hug. "I love you too, Mom."

Rob and Angel go back to his hospital room where she will spend the night. Ric drives me back to the apartment and drops me off. I sink into the couch, play with the kitties, and let this Christmas Day etch into my soul, all too aware there may not be another.

The Best Day

December 27, 2003   Westwood, California

WITH THE CANCER OUTSMARTING the oncologist's chemo and continuing its aggressive march through Rob's body, we all have some realities to face. Today Rob invites Ric and me to join him at his weekly psychotherapy session with Dr. Mauro Ferraro, who graciously opens his home office to us during his Christmas holiday. We check Rob out of the hospital and drive quietly to Westwood.

Rob makes introductions. We exchange toned-down smiles and hellos. There is a solemn air in this sunny room. Rob settles into his usual seat on the couch with a view out the sliding glass doors to the garden. I sit close, but not so close as to smother my son, even though I want so badly to hold his hand. Ric takes the chair adjacent to Mauro, facing the sofa. We are quiet, waiting. I notice a silent communication exchange between therapist and patient. Mauro nods almost imperceptively to Rob.

Rob clears his throat and begins. "There are some feelings I've been holding inside for way too long, and now it's time to let them out. Mauro's been a huge help in working with me, getting me to this point. And now that you're here, I'm just going to say this. I'm sorry if I step on feelings or hurt you, but this is important for me." Eyes down, he pauses, rattled and scared. Then the actor's confidence kicks in. He lifts his eyes and looks straight into Ric's. The only sound is the tick, tick of Mauro's clock. No one breathes.

"Dad, this is about you. I've always wanted to feel love from you, but I never have. You're distant with me. I feel ... I feel like I'm not wanted." Ric's face is expressionless, but his eyes are wide, and he's swallowing hard.

"You call me, but when we talk, I feel you have a checklist sitting in front of you with things you want to tell me, the latest jokes, and funny stories. It feels like you tick them off as you go down the list. But it's not a conversation. It's more like a stand-up routine, and you're not interacting with me.

"When we get together, you always have too many drinks, as if you need to get hammered just to be with me. Why can't we be close? Why can't you love me?"

Rob pauses and fills his lungs. His pained expression penetrates into my heart. "Dad, I need to know you love me."

I know from my own experience exactly what Rob is saying about his dad. Ric's WWII Marine father buried any emotion for his family in large amounts of alcohol. Mike was always the life of the party, a joke-meister, who used humor and booze to keep his feelings in check and relationships at a distance. It seems the demons of the father have been passed on to the son.

I can see that Ric is devastated. I know he loves Rob. I also know he doesn't have a clue how to show it. Ric rises and moves awkwardly toward Rob, like someone who has just gotten out of a full body cast and is walking for the first time in months. His face looks like a plastic mask that is about to crack. He puts his arms around Rob, stiffly at first, then he relaxes and holds him fast. The words "I love you" rise from a dusty place deep within and hit the mark. They both cry. We all cry. Even Mauro.

I shift over to Ric's chair, giving them room to be together. Ric sits next to Rob, still holding him. They begin, clumsy at first, but they look straight at each other and talk. Real talk, no jokes.

Mauro waits until they finish, then asks, "Is there anything else you want to say, Rob?"

"Just that this is the best day of my life."

CHAPTER 28

Respite

January 19, 2004   Fort Myers, Florida

MY FRIEND KATHRYN OWNS a rental house on Florida's West Coast. She recently rehabbed the aging Fifties bungalow into something right out of Architectural Digest—interior walls removed to create breezy open space, all white gourmet kitchen with high-end appliances, walls and carpets in her favorite shade of sage green accented with white floor tile, tropical plants in big natural fiber baskets, and cushy furniture that invites relaxation. Huge sliding doors open onto a cozy lanai, a swimming pool, and a backyard landscaped with robust areca palms for privacy.

"I would like to give you the house in Fort Myers for a week before you go to LA. You've been through so much, and I think this might be a good opportunity for you to rest and recover. And to fill your reserves for what's coming. You'll have to buy your own airfare, but the house is yours to use, and there's a car in the garage. The beach is only a few blocks away. Feel free to invite your boyfriend if you would like. I hope you can go."

Friends. I have the best friends ever. "Oh my gosh, yes. I can and will. Thank you! You're right. I'm a wreck and need to be somewhere quiet, beautiful, and warm where I can rest and collect myself. I'll call Tom. And ... hmmm ... this might be just the place to test out my surgically renovated feminine parts to see if they still work. Dr. D said to give it a couple months before I try, and it's been a couple months."

"Oh!" said Kathryn. "Well, I hadn't considered that, but it sounds perfect! Let me know how it goes." We both giggle like virginal teenagers.

Bags collected, Tom and I step outside the airport terminal into a gorgeous Florida afternoon. I suck in the hot humid air that goes to work immediately on my parched lungs and skin, restoring the moisture that disappeared back in November in Massachusetts when the indoor heat came on. The sun is brilliant. I laugh out loud.

A taxi carries us along streets bleached white by the intense sun. Green floral giants, normally considered potted house plants up North that need spritzing twice a week to survive, thrive here in outdoor gardens. Several varieties of ficus, night blooming jasmine, and bird of paradise tower over the single-story roof tops and flutter in the breeze. My sinuses clog a little with the perfume and pollen, but as soon as I emerge from the taxi, I stick my face into a gardenia bush at Kathryn's front door and inhale deeply. I am in horticultural heaven.

Tom drops our bags in the bedroom. We explore the house and find a bottle of champagne in the 'fridge with a note from Kathryn that says, "Good Luck!" We grab the bubbly and a couple flutes and head out the back door to the pool. He gently draws me to him, and I feel a safety I haven't felt in a long time.

We leave our clothes at the pool's edge and ease into the water, our half-empty glasses nearby. I am delighted to report that all my parts and pieces still work. Tom is delighted too.

We plan a walk on the beach after breakfast the next day. He picks up the car keys. "Let's walk," I say. "I think I'm healed enough that I'll be okay." Off we go. Five blocks later the Gulf of Mexico greets us with gentle waves brushing against white sand, sea gulls squawking as they circle picnic baskets, and a plethora of multi-colored beach umbrellas sheltering white-skinned Canadian "snowbirds" (Canadians who travel south for the winter). Shoes in hand, we make our way slowly along the water's edge to the pier, about a half mile down the beach.

"You've slowed down quite a bit and stopped talking." Tom says. "That's not like you. Are you feeling okay?"

"Maybe I need to sit down. I'm feeling some twinges."

"You stay here. I'll get the car."

"No, really, I'm fine. I can ..." Bang. Another shot of pain ricochets through my abdomen. "Okay, I'll wait here."

His eyebrows go up in alarm. "I didn't hurt you yesterday, did I?"

"I don't know what's wrong. I'll call my doctor when we get to the house."

"I'll be back as soon as I can." He kisses my forehead and runs full speed down the beach.

"Cramping and a little spotting are to be expected the first time," Dr. D reassures me. "From what you've told me, everything seems normal. Come to my office when you get home and call me if anything changes for the worse."

Nothing changes for the worse. I am hugely relieved.

Our days pass leisurely, basking in the sun, visiting lush sanctuaries, eating fresh fruits, veggies, and fish all harvested locally. Florida is working its magic, and I'm relaxed. On day five, I realize we barely have any time left. Thoughts about Rob and going to Los Angeles surface during my quiet times. They hit me hard, and my serenity goes out the window. I know what to do—take a time out and get myself back to the present moment.

I put on my swimsuit, slide into the pool, lean against the side with my face toward the sun and water lapping at my neck, close my eyes and focus on my breath. In a minute, I'm lost in meditation. My heart rate calms, my blood pressure eases, and my mind and my body drift freely into wonderland. I am once again in harmony with the world.

Somewhere on another planet, I hear footsteps. They stop at the pool's edge. "Are you all right? What's happening?"

"I'm meditating. Join me."

"I don't know what that is, but you look so peaceful. Can you teach me?"

In no time, we look like two manatees floating lazily in the water.

This beautiful week is my period of calm before the oncoming LA storm.

CHAPTER 29

The Merger

January 26, 2004   Boston, Massachusetts

LIKE CANCER, COMPANIES WANT to grow, spread into new areas and dominate. A major player in the banking world aspires to become even larger. The corporation I work for is the target.

I have known about the merger since last fall. All the belt tightening, not replacing employees who leave and piling their workloads on those who remain, smaller or no bonuses, minimal or no pay increases, and all the other employee-unfriendly measures that make our corporate books look better, have been going on for more than a year, maybe two.

There is a lot of scuttlebutt running throughout the organization about jobs and who will be in and who will be out when the merger is complete. Our HR department has five hundred nervous employees who don't know what's really going on. "Do you think we'll have to move to the new headquarters? Will you go? What kind of package do you think we'll get? When is this going down?" I'm only half tuned-in to the talk because, compared to Rob's situation, this is unimportant. Also, I'm healed enough from my surgery that I'm planning on going forward with what Rob, Angel and I discussed back in November—I'll be moving into their guest room in a few weeks because Rob's health is going downhill fast, they need extra help, and I need to be with my son.

I work out my leave of absence details, sketchy as they are, with my manager. Not trusting her to do right by me, and knowing that merger-related change will come most likely when I am in Los Angeles, I email the details to the HR Vice President. She graciously responds with words of comfort and caring for me and wishes of good health for Rob. My manager yells at me for going over her head. She says nothing about my son. I'll be glad to get away from her.

CHAPTER 30

LA Bound

February 2, 2004   Boston, Massachusetts and Los Angeles, California

I FARM MY WORKLOAD out to Susan and other HR co-workers, say farewell to friends, pack summer clothes, shut my house down to survive winter without frozen pipes, and work with Shannon to find solutions to what seem like endless loose ends. "My plants. Will you take care of my jungle of plants? Will you drive my car at least once a week? Please check the furnace. If the snow is heavy, shovel it off the decks and into the woods. Keep the bird feeder filled and make sure the squirrels haven't gotten into it. I don't know how he did it, but last week one squeezed himself inside the feeder and knocked all the seeds he didn't want out onto the ground, the little wretch." We hammer out all the details to our mutual satisfaction. I'm ready to go to LA.

I've been back and forth, Boston to Los Angeles, at least nine times since May. All good visits, but there is an ache of separation each time I fly back home and leave Rob behind. I'm about to remedy that.

· PART II ·

CALIFORNIA

CHAPTER 31

I Didn't Know

February 9, 2004   Los Angeles, California

I'M IN LA. THE office/guest room is my temporary home, a place where I can have privacy when I need it and disappear when Rob and Angel need it. I'm here as a loving mom, hausfrau, and pseudo-nurse, easing the load on Angel and their friends, especially the Core Three, who have been helping out since Rob was diagnosed. Even though love drives their behavior, the truth is, it's exhausting to be a caregiver for long periods.

In my mind, I want to make sure I don't succumb to caregiver stress, that I remain fresh and energized to help Rob. So, while he naps, I take a five-minute walk across the LA River bridge, notice the "river" has been transformed into an ugly cement canal, then bank left onto Ventura Boulevard. And voilà—there's a yoga studio. I sign up for the three-times-a-week class. The next morning, I'm lost in one hour of downward dog and sun salutations. I leave feeling serene, healthy, and ready.

Angel greets me at the door. "How was your class?" I'm surprised to see her at home.

"Wonderful."

"I hate to say this, but I really need you here 24/7 to help with Rob. Each day is different. Yesterday, he was well and cheerful. Today he's having a very hard time, so I stayed home from work. His morphine pack helps somewhat with the pain, but it leaves him spacey. He needs someone to bring water and food, help him to the bathroom, and be with him. He can't move around very well, so he's losing his muscle tone and agility. You have to be his crutch. I wish I didn't, but I need to go to work. I should have been there an hour ago. This is difficult to say—you need to be here and not at yoga."

Reality hits me hard. Yesterday's high spirits fooled me. What I really know about Rob's current condition is mostly from written updates and phone calls. I don't know the day-to-day details like holding his hand while he struggles with extreme pain, or being his physical support when he needs to move, or helping him shift his failing body in and out of the car at chemo appointments. I don't really know about all the constant and intense care required by a terminally ill person. This is new to me. I've never been in a situation like this. I'm in it now, and I'm learning fast. And I'm breaking through my armored wall of denial.

A deep maternal force gets triggered and roars up inside me. I am transformed into Supermom and ready to do everything possible to make Rob comfortable and help with housework. I start with the basics because I'm a neat freak. My own home, except for that one paperwork catchall counter in the kitchen, is well organized. I became a legend for my friend Jane when she saw my sock and underwear drawer one day. "Oh my gosh! You have everything rolled up, neatly divided and arranged by color! Let me see your closet. Good grief! Your shirts, slacks, and jackets are all separated and descend in color from dark to light! This is sick."

I get Rob settled on the couch, watching old movies, and attack the large piles of dirty clothes and linens I find stuffed into a closet. On my fourth trip up from the laundry room, Rob says, "Mom, come sit with me. Forget that for now. I want you to watch this movie with me and see this actor, who I think is terrific. It's about to start."

"I'm almost finished with this last load. I'll be right back."

Rob rolls his eyes and leans into the sofa cushions in resignation. He knows I'm driven, and it's hard to stop me when I'm engaged in a task. As I dash down the stairs, realization clobbers me hard—What on earth am I doing? I'm so caught up in clean linens that I'm missing an incredible opportunity to be with my son. Rob wants me to sit with him, and I'm putting him off. What a dope! Who knows when I'll get an opportunity like this again, if ever?

I grab the sheets from the dryer and run back to the living room, drop the basket next to the couch, and park myself gently next to him. "So, who's this actor? And why do you like him?"

He gives me a look that says, "Are you going to stay?"

I take his hand and apologize.

"His name is John Cusack. He's been acting for twenty years, doing mostly romantic comedy in teen films. Did you see *Sixteen Candles*?"

"No."

"*Stand By Me*?"

"No."

"*Broadcast News? One Crazy Summer?*"

"Nope. Nope."

"Mom, where have you been?"

"Working. Playing. Paying bills. Worrying about you."

"Gee, take some time and go to the movies." He shifts into artist mode. "There's a quality about Cusack that's romantically appealing in a Midwestern normal kid sort of way. He's quietly comedic, but he's sincere at the same time. You'll see it in him right away. He has star quality and will be a major one for sure. His sister Joan plays minor roles with him, his sister in this one. She's a real hoot. I think you're going to like this movie. It's called *Say Anything*."

The next hour and a half pass quickly. Rob comments throughout on the actor's method, timing, and delivery. "Watch this next iconic scene. Look at the way Cusack plants himself, legs wide, holding the boom box high. No dialogue, but he's speaking volumes through his body. Check out his eyes in this scene—they're incredibly expressive even though they don't move. They don't even look toward Diane's window. They just stare to the side, afraid of what he might or might not see. Look at how the makeup people darkened his eyes and brows to increase his intensity. His face seems expressionless but watch closely how he conveys his nervousness with that little jerk of his neck and the slightest twitch of his mouth. He's so good."

"I feel as if I'm sitting with Siskel or Ebert." I put my arm softly on his shoulder. "What an insider's education you've given me. Thanks, Rob, I loved the movie. You made it come alive in a new way. I'll be watching from a whole new perspective from now on."

"It's just what I do," he says, flashing a John Cusack smile.

CHAPTER 32

Resistance

February 13, 2004   Gibson Amphitheater. Universal City,
California

MONTHS AGO, WHEN THEY were sure the cancer would be past
history, Rob and Angel scored two "Chris Rock in Concert" tickets at the Gibson Amphitheater in Universal City. They were
wrong about the cancer, but nothing keeps Rob from seeing
his favorite icon of comedy.

Angel tells me what happened.

"Rob continues to refuse getting a handicap tag for the car,
so we had to park in the middle of the giant lot at the Gibson,
which meant a major hike to the theater. Then he refused to
use the wheelchair in the trunk, even though he needed it. So,
he used me for support. It took us forever to make our way
across the tarmac, up a steep incline, then up endless stairs. By
the time we got inside and found our seats, Rob could barely
walk or stay alert. He didn't say it, but I could see that walking
that far aggravated his body, and his pain was mounting. I was
worried about him, but I was also annoyed that he refused the
wheelchair.

"Throughout the show he was close to passing out. His head
tipped over the back of the chair several times and his mouth

hung open and his eyes were closed. I put my hand at the back of his neck for some stability so he wouldn't hurt himself. At one point, I thought he had died. It was awful.

"The show finally ended, and we started back to the car. He was leaning heavily on me for support. I only weigh a hundred pounds and couldn't hold him up. As we were walking down that steep incline, he stumbled and fell onto the ground near the parking lot. He just laid there, not moving. He said he hurt like hell.

"I tried like crazy, but I couldn't lift him. All these people were flooding by. I could hear them talking. They assumed he was wasted on drugs. They stepped right over him. One guy sneered and said, 'Damn druggies. You're disgusting.' I wanted to slug him.

"Well, Rob had drugs all right—morphine, strapped around his waist in an IV fanny pack. It automatically administered controlled doses to help with his pain, but his pain was so intense the morphine didn't help. Somehow, I got him to his feet and propped him up against the fence. 'I'll get one of those rickshaws to take us to the car.' I told him, 'Don't move. I'll be right back.'

"He could barely talk but managed to say, 'No Angel. I can do it. I don't need any help. I'm going to make it. I'm going to beat this cancer and be okay.'

"Oh man. It's one thing to be stoic. But it's quite another to be so stubborn that you bring harm to yourself. Pride comes before the fall. In this case, pride brought the fall, and it will happen again if he continues to resist help.

"I ran off to find a pedicab, but they were all taken. Then I spotted a man and woman stepping into the last one. I ran up to them and clamped my hand over the woman's forearm, my nails almost digging into her skin. 'Please,' I begged, crying. 'Please let me have this rickshaw for my fiancé. He really needs it.'

"'Let me go. Get away from me!' The woman tried to peel my fingers off her arm.

"'You don't understand. He has cancer and can't walk. He's in terrible shape. Look at him over there leaning on the fence. This is the last pedicab, and he really needs it. I don't know what else to do. Please.'

"When she saw Rob, she stepped out and squeezed my hand. 'Go ahead. You take it.'

"This whole night plummeted me into the depths. My hands shook as I drove us home. Rob was asleep in the passenger seat. I was on the edge of losing it. I don't know what else to do if he won't cooperate. He can be so stubborn."

I hugged Angel. "Now that I'm here, I see the awful reality of what cancer does physically and mentally to a person. I didn't fully understand before. I'm sure both Rob's refusal to talk about his cancer and his resistance to accept help are his attempts to not give in, to not succumb to what is consuming his body, to not lose what little control he has left. As an athlete, and as my son, he has learned to not accept defeat, to remain positive and hopeful in the darkest moments.

"There comes a time, however, when admitting you can't go it alone becomes an act of compassion to yourself and to others around you. There is no shame in accepting help. It takes a certain strength and humility to do that. And it allows others to give. I'm hoping this experience will help him learn that."

CHAPTER 33

No!

February 19, 2004   USC Norris Cancer Center. Los Angeles, California

THIS IS NOT A good story. Nasty red bumps the size of peas have metastasized subcutaneously in Rob's neck, his arm, and I don't know where else, but they are visible signs the cancer is spreading throughout his body.

Rob sits on the examining table. I'm standing next to him, my arm around his bony shoulders. The door opens, and Dr. L walks in. He locks eyes with Rob. He motions toward a chair in the corner, indicating I should sit down, never taking his eyes off Rob. This oncologist, who usually travels at hyper-speed, slowly lowers himself onto a padded stool. His silence is deafening.

"Rob," he begins, his voice soft and calm. "None of the chemos have worked." He pauses. "We have run out of things to try. This is an aggressive cancer, and it is moving quickly through your body." He pauses again, this time longer. "This is never easy to say. Rob, the way this cancer is traveling, I estimate you have less than a year to live. You need to get your affairs in order. I suggest you contact hospice."

Rob is silent. He swallows hard and wipes his eyes with his shirtsleeve. He tries but can't hold back the tears. "I can't believe this. I'm getting married in Prague next year. I want to live. I have to live. What are you saying?"

"I'm so sorry, Rob. Your body is strong, and you are a fighter. That has helped you survive as long as you have. The chemos we used were so powerful they would have killed anyone else long ago, but you have tolerated them. The awful part is they didn't work.

"It's time for hospice now. They will provide a team-centered approach to end of life issues—pain management, emotional support for you and your family, coaching for your family on how to care for you, grief counseling. They'll supply a hospital bed for your home. They are dedicated and available 24/7. However, most families are in denial and wait too long to call them. I suggest you contact them today. I'll walk with you to the desk where they have the information you'll need." He helps Rob down from the examination table, puts his arm around Rob's shoulders, and opens the grey steel door.

I become nauseous, gag, and nearly spew the contents of my acidic stomach on the floor. Those words, "less than a year to live," from the man in charge of Rob's recovery, smack me soundly across the face. Wake up to the reality of your child's impending death, he's telling me.

I can't. I can't accept it. I won't let it in. My inner keyboard deletes this information immediately. I won't hear it. I won't even consider losing Rob. There is a miracle waiting. I know it. I tell God we don't need a big dramatic miracle, just a quiet one. One in which Rob wakes up in the morning and knows something is different—the pain is gone, the red bumps are gone, the cancer is gone. Please God. Just a little miracle.

CHAPTER 34

Chemo

February 20, 2004   USC Norris Cancer Center. Los Angeles, California

"I'M GETTING JUICED AT 10:30 today, Mom. We'll have to leave by 9:45. Are you ready?"

We've ignored Dr. L's hospice instruction. It's chemo day as usual. Rob eases gently into the passenger seat. I'm the chauffeur. Not accustomed to LA traffic, and because I'm carrying precious cargo, I drive slowly for the first five minutes. I check my rearview and side mirrors excessively. As I accelerate and brake ad nauseam toward the UC Norris Cancer Center, Rob remains quiet until a Beemer cuts in front of us, then slams on his brakes. "Ahhh!" he shouts and grabs for the oh-shit handle. No problem. I now understand how to change lanes in LA—put your turn signal on, floor it, and go. I've been driving in Boston for thirty years, which qualifies me for the Grand Prix.

Rob steps slowly into the outpatient infusion center. The nurse behind the desk sees him and smiles. "Hi, Rob. How're ya doin'? Who's this with you? Has to be your mom." Chatting away, she leads him to a row of pale green chairs that look a lot like something you'd find in a hair salon. The three-tiered cart on wheels, usually filled with brushes, clips and hair goop, holds tubes, needles, and a clear bag filled with poison that will soon flow through his veins. He relaxes into the chair, puts in his ear buds, and disappears into a Grateful Dead concert. Pale green curtains on stainless steel rods separate each patient station. "Do you want the drape open or closed?" she mouths silently as if she is addressing a deaf person.

"Closed," he says in an overly loud voice, not realizing Jerry Garcia has raised the sound bar, and he's speaking above it.

This reminds me of one of our Disney World/Red Sox Spring Training vacations when Rob was eight. On the plane from Boston to Orlando, he put his headphones on and became one with the music, tapping his foot, bobbing his head in time with the beat, and humming. I guess Kenny Rogers took him into a place of musical ecstasy because he burst out singing in a voice louder than he realized, "You picked a fine time to leave me Lucille. Four hundred children and a crop in the field ..." Laughter erupted from the passengers nearby.

Rob lifted one headphone speaker from his ear closest to me. "What's so funny?"

"It's four *hungry* children, not four hundred children," I told him.

"Ohhh. That makes more sense."

I smiled at this little man who would become the lead singer in a rock band in seventeen years.

The nurse prepares his dose and hooks it up to the catheter in his chest, which goes directly into his heart. A couple months ago, this port became infected, a fairly common occurrence I'm told. His temperature spiked, and the pain was agonizing. A hospital stay, antibiotics, and a fresh port took care of it. Good god, what he's been through.

I watch him closely over the next hour, not sure if he's sleeping or chilling out. I study his emaciated body, drawn cheeks, scraggly hair stub, and marvel that he is so peaceful. Clearly this chemo is routine for him. For me, I'm almost to the bottom of my Kleenex box.

"What's it like?" I ask on the way home.

He speaks as if his batteries are running low. "It burns a little at first, but then it eases up. The music helps distract me. I'm lucky I don't get nauseous. Lots of people do, but this blend is okay for me." He stops, closes his eyes, and nearly falls asleep, then jerks awake. "The worst part is how exhausted I feel afterwards. Not just tired, but I feel like I weigh five hundred pounds. Moving is difficult. Everything is difficult. I just want to sleep forever. I'll conk out when we get home and be out the rest of the day and most of tomorrow."

Tomorrow! Tomorrow night is his surprise thirty-fifth birthday party.

CHAPTER 35

Celebration

February 21, 2004   Studio City, California

INTIMACY, THE KIND THAT emerges when conditions are extreme, is all around Rob tonight as his dearest friends celebrate the close of his thirty-fifth year. The Core Four are on the couch with arms around each other exchanging Our Boy Mulloy stories from their years together at USC, cattle calls for parts in plays and commercials, and meeting and loving the women in their lives.

There is a brotherhood in the air that is almost palpable. The trials of disease have flown away during these few hours of camaraderie. Rob is deeply happy.

CHAPTER 36

Surprise

February 22, 2004   Los Angeles, California

FRIDAY NIGHT'S PARTY WAS a subterfuge. Angel planned it to throw Rob off the scent of the real surprise party tonight at the No Bar in North Hollywood. How kind of the club owner to offer his venue gratis. Everyone loves Rob. Over one hundred people RSVP'd, including Tasha, a high school friend of Rob's from Massachusetts, and Shannon, his sister who flew in last night and stayed with her dad at the Hilton around the corner.

I can't help but think about how friends make a huge effort to come from far and wide for a funeral, but it's too late for the deceased to know how many people care enough about him to do this. A funeral is for the survivors. This birthday event is giving everyone, including Rob, the opportunity to celebrate his life, their relationship with him, and unspoken but obvious, to say goodbye.

Angel and I sort out the "get Rob to the party" details down to the minute. Angel calls Jay, Rob's regular Sunday night card-playing buddy, to get him in on the plan. First, Angel will leave the apartment at 6:00 to "have sushi and hang out with her girlfriends," but really will go to the club to make sure the food is ready, drinks are flowing, and the DJ is doing his thing.

Then Jay will arrive at 6:40 to pick Rob up for a "poker tournament" at the No Bar. They will linger until I depart at 6:45 "to meet a Boston friend who now lives in Laguna," but I really will go to the club like Paul Revere and call out, "Rob is coming! Rob is coming!" and move the stragglers inside from the parking lot and quiet them down for the big "Surprise! Happy Birthday!"

Perfect.

Not so perfect. Jay arrives. "This is going to be a super night. I'm feeling lucky. How about you, Mulloy? You're the poker stud. Ready to win some cash?"

"I'm not going, Jay. I don't feel up to it. The chemo. You know. I'm going to bed."

Jay and I turn white. A pregnant pause fills the space between us. I jump in with mumbo jumbo. "You might feel better if you get out and occupy your mind with something you love. You've played in all those tournaments in Vegas. I think you should go."

"Nah. I really don't feel well."

What a moral dilemma. The poor guy feels terrible. He's dying. And we're trying to rally him to go to a huge party.

Jay pipes in. "I'll tell you what, Rob. Let's go anyway. We'll play a couple hands and if you still don't feel well, I'll bring you home. I promise. All you have to do is give me the high sign. Whaddaya think?"

"Yeah, okay. Let's go."

"Oh! I'll be late if I don't go now. Have fun guys!" I dash toward the door. Jay suddenly has to use the bathroom but is really giving me time for a head start so I can get to the No Bar and prepare the revelers.

My every thought about Rob is tinged with worry. I'm acutely aware he doesn't want to be out tonight. The "What if's" are strong—what if this is too much for him? What if someone has the flu and Rob gets it? What if ...

Jay steps back and lets Rob walk through the club doors first. A blast of cheers, whistles, and "Happy Birthdays!" nearly knock him over. He reels back, overwhelmed. Jay is at his side to steady him and draw him into the room where friends from every part of his life—family, high school, USC, acting, swim team, music, poker, weekend hang outs—surround him.

He's modest in his response, quiet, and deeply touched. "I don't know what to say ... for the first time in my life." His eyes are moist as he scans the crowd.

"Oh my god, Tasha! What are you doing here? You live in Boston!" He moves in for a hug. "And Cyn! And ..."

Rob, the star in the room, rises briefly to the occasion. A wry smile appears on his face. When the timing is just right, he calls out, "You mean to tell me there's no poker tonight? Pfft. That's it. I'm going home!" He does an exaggerated walk toward the door. The crowd laughs out loud.

"Meet me in the back room, Mulloy. I'll be happy to take your money!" someone calls.

"I'm feeling a full house around me!" another voice offers.

Groans and chuckles.

"Yeah, yeah, I'll flush you all right off the table," Rob fires back. Laughter fills the room.

Music blares, and the party begins in earnest. Someone hands him a pilsner, his favorite.

Twenty minutes pass, and I can see Rob is weary. I've been talking to the guests, but always with an eye on him. He needs to sit down. He tries to avoid the high fives and hugs that are coming at him from those who are not fully in tune with how desperately fragile he is, or how a well-meaning touch causes extreme pain. Rich steps in to run interference as Angel guides him to the leather banquette that curves around the far side of the room. Here he holds court for the rest of the evening as friends move in and away, in and away.

A loud tap, tap from the speakers silences the group and the lights dim. Rich's voice directs attention toward the kitchen where Angel is wheeling out a humongous banana cream cake, a true work of art from a bakery frequented by Hollywood celebrities. The blaze from thirty-five candles casts a warm glow over Angel's face as she moves the sculptured four-hundred-dollar pastry toward Rob. Someone says, "Oh my god, that's a Sweet Lady Jane cake!" and the crowd murmurs its approval.

"I need some help here, guys," Rob says, his eyes bright. The Core Three surround the table and blow on the candles at the same time as Rob, knowing he doesn't have it in him to extinguish the flames alone.

Angel serves the cake. Rob is exhausted and close to passing out from the pain. In a voice barely audible, he addresses the crowd, breathless. "I have to leave. Please stay and have fun. This was great. I love you."

Rich and Jay help him to the car. Angel drives him home.

He is gone, but the party goes on.

CHAPTER 37

A Very Special Birthday

February 24, 2004   Studio City, California

"WE'VE DECIDED NOT TO wait any longer. We're getting married today!" Angel announces over late morning coffee. "It's Rob's birthday, and we thought this would be a very special day to celebrate with a wedding."

Angel wastes no time. She locates and books a chapel. "California doesn't require blood tests, and we have the license."

"What about a wedding ring?" I ask.

She stops. "Strangely enough, we already have Rob's ring. We were going to shop for mine when he was healthy again. Oh, no. How on earth can I find a wedding ring in three hours?"

"Are there any antique jewelry stores nearby?" Shannon asks.

Angel brightens. "Yes! What a great idea. The Antique Mall on Ventura. Shannon, will you go with me to help pick one out? Ellyn and Ric, you're taking Rob to his therapy appointment with Mauro at eleven, so your job is to deliver the groom to the wedding chapel at one o'clock."

"What about a wedding dress? Do you have one?"

"No dress. This will be super casual. My red jeans and a white sweater. Rob will be in his usual jeans and tee shirt."

Angel springs into a flurry of phone calls, inviting family and friends.

The wedding news thrills Mauro. Rob is a nervous husband-to-be, jittery with the commitment he is about to make. Even though ...

We're stuck in a huge LA traffic snarl. Time ticks away as we sit in Rob's Honda, helpless, unable to move forward. Ric's at the wheel, Rob is shotgun, and I'm in the back seat. We're already half an hour late. Rob calls Angel. "Just wanted you to know I'm not on my way to Tijuana. There's an accident on the 10. It might take another half hour to get through. I'm so sorry, honey. Hold tight and wait for me. I love you."

He signs off just as the fistula on his abdomen, an unhealed leftover from a post-surgery feeding tube, decides to spurt out part of today's lunch. Smelly spinach-green goo spreads across the bottom of his shirt. He's already a wreck, and this vile insult from his already failing body takes him to the edge. His hands shake and tears form in his eyes. "What am I going to do? I can't get married with this crap all over me."

I rest my hand affectionately on his shoulder, then touch his cheek. "We can fix this. Is there something like a Target nearby? You guys wait in the car. I'll run in and get a package of moist wipes, fresh bandages, and a new tee shirt. I won't be but a few minutes. You can get cleaned up and change while Dad drives. No one will ever know this happened."

It's nearly two o'clock when we arrive at the chapel. Angel is near frantic. Late for his wedding, Rob is rattled and fears another fistula disaster. They hug and settle each other down as the rest of us find a seat.

The minister begins the ceremony as Rob and Angel stand before him. He talks on, and on, and on, waxing gloriously about the sanctity of marriage and blah, blah, blah. After ten minutes, Rob wobbles. He has been standing far too long, and his deteriorating body cannot support him much longer. Angel puts her arm around his waist, and he leans into her so he won't fall. Hasn't anyone told the minister? He's oblivious to what's happening to the groom and rattles on. Ric walks up to the altar and puts his arm around Rob, holding him steady.

Finally, they exchange rings, kiss, and Ric all but carries Rob to a seat where he collapses. A sweet smile lights up his weary face. "I'm a husband," he says. "And Angel is my wife."

A year ago, they planned a glamorous wedding in Prague at the Old Town Hall, a gorgeous Fifteenth century venue, "with a jubilant shindig to follow," the invitation said. This is not that glamorous wedding, but it is a marriage, and Angel is content that this man, who has been her boyfriend and fiancé for four years, is now her husband.

We are happy for them in a bittersweet way.

CHAPTER 38

Coma

February 27, 2004   Studio City, California

THE CORE FOUR SPREAD out across Rob and Angel's living room, laughing at Ben Stiller's antics in *Zoolander*, one of Rob's comedy favorites. Wrapped in a blanket in the recliner, Rob is apparently happy and pain free as he yucks it up with his friends.

This scenario reminds me of Norman Cousins, who discovered a correlation between laughter and pain relief. He had a rare joint disease that left him in constant debilitating agony. He loved Marx Brothers' movies and found that "Ten minutes of good belly laughter gives me two hours of pain-free sleep. It creates a body anesthesia, so I don't need any morphine." It seems to be working for Rob.

But now at ten a.m. he is tired and excuses himself to the bedroom. The gang is used to his fatigue. They order Chinese food and hang out while he rests.

Two hours later Angel checks on Rob. She runs out of the bedroom in a panic. "I can't wake him up! He's not responding!"

We all rush into the bedroom. There he is on the king-sized bed, absolutely still, eyes closed, breath barely there and ragged. He looks totally peaceful. Someone lifts Rob's eyelids. His eyes are rolled back in his head and everyone gasps. We try to decide if this is normal or not while Angel calls the doctor. He tells us we can either call 911 and get him to a hospital or keep him at home and let him die peacefully without the invasion of medical intervention. We choose to keep him at home.

Dr. L told us last week that Rob's situation is very serious (he even used the word grim), and we should get all affairs in order. And Rob told us, in a series of very intense discussions, that he wants to die at home surrounded by friends.

I'm traumatized. Frantically I call Ric, who just flew home to Seattle last night. "You have to come back to LA. Something has happened to Rob. He's in a coma, not responding. This could be it, Ric. He might die tonight. You've got to come."

"I'm on my way. I'll be on the next flight to LA."

Hours pass as nine of us sit around Rob's bed. *American Beauty*, his favorite Grateful Dead album, plays over and over and over and over and over until we all hate the music, but we know he loves it. We hope he is hearing it wherever he is, so we tune it out and focus on him.

At seven-thirty p.m. I see Ric through the bedroom window, rushing up the sidewalk to the front door. He reaches out and puts his hand on the doorknob. At that precise moment, Rob wakes up. His eyes are bright, he's smiling. He cracks few jokes.

"Hey!" Rob says. "What are you all doing in my bedroom? Waiting for me to kick it?"

Everyone is thrown off balance. Yes, we actually are, but a chorus of cover-ups ensues. "Huh, no, of course not. We're waiting for you to wake up."

"We just wanted to make sure you're okay."

"Uh, um. How are you feeling, Rob?"

Ric walks into the room.-"Dad, what are you doing here? You just left."

Now Ric is thrown off balance. "I heard you weren't doing well, and I wanted to be here for you."

"Well, as long as everybody is here, and my favorite band is singing, let's play a game! How about Cranium?"

We're stupefied into silence.

"Cranium anyone? Do you know how to play, Mom?"

"Uh, no, I don't."

"Well, how about if you throw the dice for the players?"

"Sure." I'm still knocked off my pins by this dramatic turn-around. It's as if he is perfectly fine. The old Rob is back.

The board game begins. I don't understand what's going on, but I seem to roll the right numbers because there is a lot of cheering. At some point I step back, and the real game players go to town for the next hour. Ric and I retreat to the chairs in the corner. Everyone else is on the bed. He gives me the wide-eyed, "What's going on?" look. I shrug back at him, clueless.

"Hey, I'm hungry! Is there any Chinese left?" Rob calls out. "Let's go to the living room and drink some beer and eat some food!"

Angel, bewildered, whispers to me, "What's happening?"

"I have no idea. But it's wonderful!" I whisper back.

Rob is walking with a bounce in his step, like he just emerged from a swimming pool having won a big race. His energy is high. His mind is sharp. The Rob smile is in full force.

Is this the miracle we've all been praying for? Has there been a divine intervention, and now he is healthy again?

The entourage moves to the living room, exchanging confused looks. Rob holds court and entertains us for another forty-five minutes.

As quickly as the miracle came, that's how quickly it leaves. He slumps in his chair. "I'm really tired. I'm going back to bed."

CHAPTER 39

Where Are You?

February 28, 2004   USC Norris Cancer Center. Los Angeles, California

WE ARRIVE AT THE hospital for another round of chemo, but Rob is so ill, so unable to move on his own, so on the verge of passing out, the lab nurse calls Dr. L. A gurney arrives in minutes. The orderlies pluck Rob from the chemo lab and get him settled in a private hospital bed where he immediately disappears into another coma. His body is here, he is still breathing, but the charismatic Rob Mulloy I know and love is clearly not in residence.

I believe we each have a soul, a consciousness, a separate part of us that merges with a physical body in this lifetime. How it gets here, where it comes from, is undetermined in my mind. That's not important. What it does while it's here is important. Do we come with an agenda, a bucket list of things to accomplish or overcome, then leave when it's complete? I don't really know. Maybe I'll find out when I die. Maybe I won't.

What I want to know is—while Rob is in this coma, where is he?

Our minds are set up to make sense of, to have an explanation for the incomprehensible. Is spirituality one of those things man created so we can live more peaceably and not go crazy existentially? I don't know that either. But today, here in Rob's private room, I want to know if his soul is out talking with someone on a different plane of existence. Is he discussing his agenda, the Rob Mulloy Life Bucket List? I imagine the conversation.

Rob begins. "In my thirty-five years I've completed and checked off items one through five. Six is, well, mostly done. Can I get partial credit for that? Seven. Whoa, that was a doozy, but I got through. Eight, nine. Done and done. Ten. Life Commitment to Another Person. That was the big one for me. And, you know, now that it's done, now that I'm a married man, I realize there was no reason to be afraid. In fact, it's totally cool. So, that's my list. Am I finished now, or what?"

My bizarre reverie evaporates as Dr. L enters the room. He walks over to Rob and pats him sweetly on the shoulder. He's gentle in the delivery of his message, but adamant in his intension. "No more chemo for this guy."

"But, but his cell count is up four points!" Angel fires back.

"It may be up four points, but from where? His blood count is dangerously low, even with the four points. I'm so sorry, Angel, but it's time to face the hard facts. Rob has only days left. It's time for hospice." His steely blue eyes hold Angel's, making sure his communication is clear and will not be disregarded again. His voice softens. "I'll arrange it for you. Today." He exits the room slowly. His usual super-charged persona subdued.

We are quiet as we let the dark truth slip in. "... only days left." The mental barriers to bad news that I set up months ago begin to crumble and fall away. Suddenly the room feels frigid. I pull my sweater around me and hold myself tight. Angel squeezes herself onto the hospital bed next to Rob and puts her arms around him. "Where are you?" she whispers, her head nuzzled into his neck. Her new wedding ring, with four little diamonds, one for each year they've been together, flashes rainbows across the crispy white sheets.

"How's our patient today?" chirps the floor nurse as she walks into the room.

"Anna!" Angel recognizes the nurse who has been with them over the past few months. "It's not good, Anna. Rob's in a coma. Dr. L says hospice."

"I'm so sorry. I always love having you guys in my ward. You've been such fun, even in the hard times. I'm here to do anything I can to help. How about something to snack on? There's no telling how long he'll be in this, or how long you'll be here." She checks Rob's vitals. "He's steady. I'll be right back."

Anna returns with an armload of graham crackers and apple juice in sippy cartons. She puts two extra pillows on the end of the bed. "In case those chairs get too hard."

"We got married four days ago," Angel offers.

"That's awesome! Tell me about it. Let's see your ring. Oh, it's beautiful!"

The two of them launch into girl talk. Angel's spirits rise a bit, and she's temporarily distracted by conversation. Anna announces she's pregnant. "We've been trying for so long. We almost gave up. But finally, it worked! We're so happy! The baby is due in July." They carry on with baby talk.

Six hours pass with Anna popping in and out of the room. Rob remains ... gone. In the seventh hour, he stirs. Angel, Anna, and I chime out, "Welcome back, Rob!"

He's groggy. His eyes won't focus. "Where ... Where am I?" He looks around the room. "How did I get here? What happened?"

"You're in the hospital. You were in another coma and were out for almost seven hours," Angel tells him.

"What? I don't remember ... Wait a minute ..." he stumbles over his words. He's not fully back into his consciousness yet. Words come hard. "What ... What did I ... hear?" He shakes his head as if to clear it and looks at Angel with a confused smile. "Are we ... pregnant? Are we having ... a baby ... in July?"

Angel falters, then gathers her composure. She speaks gently to him. "No, honey. It's Anna who's having the baby in July. We aren't pregnant."

"But I heard you say ..."

"No, Honey. You heard Anna."

"Oh. I thought for sure it was us."

Dr. L releases him two hours later. It takes a couple orderlies to lift him out of the wheelchair and into the car. His mind is coming back, but his body is not. The ride home is quiet.

I'm curious for first-hand information about "the other side" and want to learn more about my son's out-of-body experience. "Rob, you were in a coma for most of the day. Do you have any memory of where you were? What was it like? What do you remember?"

"I don't want to talk about it," he says with such finality that I let it go. I'm not sure why he won't talk. Could be he refuses to weaken his resolve about getting better. Could be it was so profound, it can't be described. Could be it was just darkness, and there's nothing to say.

But he heard us while in the coma. On some level of awareness, he caught the baby conversation. Fascinating. Researchers say, and this experience shows, that family should talk to their loved ones while unconscious because they can hear. (So, keep it positive and be careful what you say.)

I open the door to the apartment. Angel wheels Rob in. They both stop talking. All the furniture has been moved around, and in the center of the living room is a hospital bed fully made up with sheets, pillows, and a white blanket.

"What's this?" Rob is angry. Angel picks up some paperwork from hospice, and a note from the landlord saying they let the delivery guys in per Angel's instructions.

"Dr. L ordered hospice for you. He wants you to have the best palliative care now that chemo is over. So, I approved it. I didn't realize it would get here so fast."

"What do you mean 'chemo is over?' I don't agree to this. I don't want hospice. I can still be useful. I can still enjoy life."

Rob struggles to lift himself out of the wheelchair. He shuffles with great difficulty to the French doors, opens them, and steps carefully out onto the small balcony. "I can still enjoy life," he whispers, desperate.

Little does he know this is the last time he will ever be mobile.

We help him to the bed.

CHAPTER 40

Hospice

February 29, 2004   Studio City, California

CHARLOTTE, THE HOSPICE NURSE, sits at the dining table with Angel, Ric, and me. Rob is in a drugged sleep only fifteen feet away in the heart of the living room. I'm nervous he can hear us, but Charlotte says, "One of hospice's principles is being open and honest. I know this is a very difficult situation for you, but it's easier if you can let go of denial. I'm here to provide quality end-of-life care for all of you in the family unit."

She describes the services she and her team will manage. "Rob will not be in pain. Palliative care means he will have relief with drugs appropriate for his situation. For him, it's a morphine drip with a locked time-release attached to the side of his hospital bed. A nurse will come in every other day to bathe him and change the sheets."

The list of services is impressive. Charlotte describes what will happen in Rob's last moments of life. She explains the horrible Cheyne-Stokes breathing, also known as "the death rattle," or end stage breathing, when the body is shutting down. "The sound will most likely drive you absolutely insane, but know at that point he is not suffering. He is moving toward peace." She says words that land hard on my ears—death, wills, removal of the body, funeral director, cremation. Oh, my god. And she emphasizes again that she is here for all of us 24/7. "You can call me at 3 a.m. if you are scared, have a question, or just want to talk."

"Why didn't we do this sooner?" I ask no one in particular.

"This is what most families say when they finally realize how much hospice actually does to bring meaningful and compassionate care and dignity to the end of life. I am here to make Rob's transition as pain free physically, emotionally, socially, and spiritually as possible. And don't worry, there is no cost. Medicare Hospice Benefit legislation passed back in 1982. It gives federal funds for hospice care for every citizen, regardless of their ability to pay.

"But most people hear hospice, and they shut down. They refuse to acknowledge their loved one is going to die. So, they wait until the very end to call us. They don't know about all the services we could have provided up to this point."

"That would be us," I say. "It's nearly impossible for any of us to admit that Rob is dying." I lose it and sob. "This is the first time I've said it—Rob is dying."

"Tell me about Rob and his life," she asks with genuine interest.

The next hour is a recap of the life Rob lived to the hilt. Charlotte digs deep. She asks questions to better understand who he is. She's amazing.

"Why do you do this kind of work? I would think it would be so difficult," I ask.

"I lost my daughter, Janine, to cancer twenty years ago. I was so grateful to hospice and decided this would be my way to honor her memory and to help other families who are going through the difficult time I experienced."

A tear rolls down Charlotte's cheek. "I'm so sorry. This is not about me. I'm usually not asked that question. You caught me off guard. But you can see that even after twenty years, grief lingers. Time heals, but it never goes away entirely. Rob will be in your hearts always. I'm here to help you make his transition as positive as possible.

"I have some supplies to bring in from my car. Would you like to help?"

Charlotte opens her trunk. I blink at what I see. Neatly arranged in multiple plastic tubs is a complete pharmacy. She piles sterile pads, adult diapers, medical gizmos, and tubing into my arms. She grabs an armload of I have no idea what and we head for the apartment.

"Wow," is all I can say.

"Amazing isn't it? I have everything Rob will possibly need right here in my trunk."

CHAPTER 41

A Blur

February 29–March 3, 2004   Studio City, California

I'M SO OUT OF my mind with panic over these next few days, I can't remember the flow of activities that takes place. I only know my heart is racing out of control and my brain is frantic, trying to figure out something, anything to save my son, but there's not a damned thing I can do. Rob is slipping away quietly.

I have only freeze-frame memories of these four days—Charlotte coming and going, refreshing his morphine and upping the dosage each day to a level that numbs his excruciating pain. She watches his heart monitor, checks his body. Then she sits with each of us, holding our hands, encouraging us to speak our feelings and cry or rant. "If you keep your feelings in, it's not healthy." I don't remember what I say, or if I say anything. The closer Rob gets to death, the tighter I hold on to denial. It's like being in the middle of an inferno, trapped in a building engulfed in flames. I know there is no escape route, yet I continue to eat my dinner, then do the dishes. Crazy. I can feel the flames of death nearby, but I continue to hope they will miraculously go away. Complete denial.

One day starts with a disaster. The Core Three, Rich Speight, JT Guerin, and Rob Boltin, have been with him daily for ten months, catering to his every need, helping in ways I don't even know about. Today Rob can no longer walk by himself, his legs barely work, so they all but carry him a few steps away to the commode behind a screen. Another in a long series of "lasts" occurs—his body evacuates everything, he is empty. The guys clean him up and maneuver him gently back to the hospital bed. Angel's sister Heather, a nurse, and I take the waste bucket to the bathroom.

"I'll add some warm water from the tub. It will make it easier to pour it all down the toilet," she says. As she hands the bucket to me, it slips from her fingers, and the contents pour onto the floor and spatter the walls and my shoes.

"Oh, my god!" she shrieks. In spite of the fact she works in a cancer ward, she is both mortified and grossed out.

"If you get something to clean this up, I'll take care of it," I offer.

"Really? You'll do that?"

"Yes, I will. Just don't let anyone out there know what's going on in here."

She scurries away. This is not too different from Rob's first year of life. It reminds me of the night his cries woke Ric and me at 3 a.m. Somehow, he got both his jammies and his diaper off and had smeared poop all over his body and all over his crib. He grinned when we rushed into his room. That was a tough clean up, but an act of parental love, as is this.

The next day, it's clear Rob can no longer get up to use the commode, and because he is no longer eating solids, just liquids, Charlotte explains it's time for a catheter. She carefully inserts it up through his penis and into his bladder. The intense pain cuts through Rob's morphine fog. He screams and passes out. I die a little.

Petok and Xaoxao, Angel's two black kitties are vigilant. Petok hops gently onto the bed and curls up on the sheet between Rob's knees. She remains "on duty" for a few hours, then jumps down to the floor. Xaoxao is there waiting for her turn. She leaps up and settles into the same spot for another few hours. The two of them, who Rob and Angel collectively call the Peewoos, take turns watching over Rob so he is never alone. They do this rotation every three hours, day and night.

Rob's kitty, DeNiro, is showing signs of stress. He's not very social anyway, so all the activity, the strangeness of this new bed, all these people, and Rob not responsive to him, sends him to hiding in the corner of the living room behind the ficus tree, where he occasionally peeks out to see if things have returned to normal.

Thank goodness for the Core Three. These guys have been on the scene since the coma and Cranium game day. They have been his lifeline, his daily caregivers, and comfort providers since he got sick ten months ago. I'm amazed now as they step in and take charge of details like feeding us, running errands, and organizing home and visitors, which leave us time to sit with him, hold his hand, and give and receive little Rob kisses that are oh so very meaningful and sweet.

The Boltins live across the courtyard. Their apartment becomes the "I need a break" place, the food kitchen, and overnight quarters for the Guerin's and the Speight's. They are all sitting around Rob, who is in another drugged sleep, when the aide comes to bathe him. He's dressed only in a tee shirt that Charlotte tore all the way down the back so it will cover his upper body without hurting him. A sheet covers the rest of his unclothed body. She is discreet in her routine, but as she lifts the sheet to bathe his lower body, shock fills the room.

Rob's testicles are swollen to the size of grapefruits. Boltin unconsciously grabs his own and almost gets sick. Fortunately, hospice nurse Charlotte is there. "Rob's body is shutting down," she explains. "It's no longer processing fluids, which is causing the swelling all over his body. It's extremely painful, but he's not feeling it at all because of the morphine."

Boltin and Speight move the couch so it rests next to Rob's hospital bed. Angel piles it with pillows so it's on an equal level with the bed. She spends each night sleeping next to him. We take turns lying next to him during the day, talking quietly, saying the things we need to say before he goes. He is not awake most of time, but we talk to him anyway. I take his hand, pull myself close to his ear and whisper, "Rob, before you were born, my life lacked purpose and direction. When you were born, you gave my life purpose and direction. You gave my life meaning, real meaning, for the first time. I thank you for that very wonderful gift. I loved you from your very first breath. I will always love you."

When he is awake, I tell him, "I know I made mistakes raising you. I did and said some stupid things in moments of frustration, and I have a lot of guilt. Can you ever forgive me?"

His voice is barely there. "Mom, there's nothing to forgive. You did the best you knew how. There's nothing to forgive."

My guilt only intensifies, remembering every time I lost my temper, wasn't as attentive as I should have been, said words that hurt. Those little moments seem huge now.

"I love you, Rob."

"I love you too, Mom."

Because his body is shutting down, his ability to swallow is compromised, and he can only take liquids offered on a pink sponge attached to a small plastic stick. We dip the sponge into water, place it on his tongue. He can barely suck the liquid out of it. He whispers to me, "I want some beer."

I get flustered, not sure how beer will interact with the intense medication. Charlotte sits nearby. I turn toward her and mouth, "Is it okay to give him beer?"

The look she gives me brings me back to reality. "Does it really make a difference at this point?" she asks.

Someone pours a pilsner into a small bowl. The pink sponge sops it up. Rob lets the golden brew drip down his throat, a weak smile on his face.

This is the last sustenance he takes in.

He looks at me, only able to move his eyes. "I'm fighting. I'm fighting," he whispers. His eyes shift to Angel, and he mouths, "I love you."

These are the last words he ever speaks as he slips into his final coma.

CHAPTER 42

Death

Thursday, March 4, 2004   Studio City, California

CHARLOTTE IS RIGHT ABOUT the Cheyne-Stokes breathing. It's horrible. An unnerving rattling sound accompanies each strained breath. Slowly in. Rattle. Slowly out. Rattle, rattle. Without warning, Rob's breathing stops. An eternity passes. Then a desperate gasp for air follows as he fills his lungs. He pants. The pattern repeats. And repeats.

Angel, the Speights, Guerins, Boltins, Angel's sister Heather, Ric and I hover around Rob. Hours pass. His unconscious and desperate struggle to breathe is the only sound in the room. We take each breath with him, then hold ours when his stops.

Angel can't take it any longer. The group escorts her to the Boltin's, leaving Ric and me alone with our son. We pull our chairs up close. We each hold one of his hands, honoring his request to do so when the end is near.

Dinner comes and goes. Neither of us has any appetite. Someone brings us a bottle of pinot noir and two glasses. Ric opens it and pours. "To our wonderful son, Rob," he says. His glass hovers over Rob's chest.

I meet it with a gentle clink. "To Rob, who I love with all my heart."

This small action somehow bridges the gap between two people who have been divorced for over twenty years. It reconnects us to a gentler time.

"Remember when we used to call him The Bear?" Ric asks.

"Yes, I do. We called him Ro-bear, with a French accent, then shortened it to Bear, then The Bear. He had that little yellow one-piece outfit with a red teddy bear patch on it. He was so cute. Do you remember when he was eighteen months old, and out of the blue, he started to whistle?" We each imitate the whistle and laugh.

"What about when he used to sing "Aquarius" from his stroller? 'When the moon is in the seventh house and Jupiter aligns with Mars.' People would stop and listen, fascinated. It was his first performance. What an adorable kid he was."

We carry on like this for at least an hour, sharing fond memories, stopping mid-word each time Rob's breathing stops. Then we're quiet, but only on the outside. My mind is wild, my heart racing. I vacillate between fond memories and sheer panic. I can't stand the intensity of the Cheyne-Stokes any longer. Just as my body starts to shake, and I'm about to lose my mind, my cell phone rings. It's Charlotte, the hospice nurse.

"What's going on?" she asks.

"He's been in Cheyne-Stokes all day. Now that it's night, the gaps between breaths have lengthened. Sometimes it's almost two minutes between breaths. You were right, I can't bear this. It sounds like he's struggling. I think he's gone, then I hear his frantic gasp for breath like he's desperate to hang on to life. Then he stops breathing, and I think he's gone again. I'm losing it, Charlotte. I don't think I can take anymore. I want to run out of the room, but I want to be with him in case ..."

"Something told me to call you. I had a feeling you were having a very hard time. Even though Rob sounds like he's struggling, remember, he feels nothing in this state. He is actually very peaceful."

"What can we do?" I ask. "I feel so helpless. We all feel so helpless watching him try to breathe. It's hard to believe that he's at peace. It sounds so horrific, so desperate."

"There is nothing you can do. Again, Rob is comfortable and not feeling anything right now. He's preparing to go."

"Oh, my god. Are you sure there's nothing we can do to help him?"

She is silent for what seems like a long time.

"Charlotte, are you there?"

"I'm not telling you this, but there is something you can do, if you choose to. It's something to discuss with Angel and Ric. You need to decide together. You didn't hear this from me, but if you want to help him leave, to help him come to the end of his life, there is a release on the morphine drip lock."

She gives me detailed instructions on how to let the morphine flow freely. "This will help him along to the end."

I thank her, sign off, and sit there, stunned, unable to speak. Finally, I tell Ric.

Speight comes into the apartment to check on Rob.

"I think it's time for Angel to be here," I tell him. "The gap between his breaths is getting longer. It could be any time." I choke on my words.

The whole group of dear friends brings Angel into the bedroom. They find places to settle in and wait. Angel sits next to Ric. They share Rob's left hand. I hold his right hand.

I sit with Ric's and my secret.

I'm numb and agitated at the same time. I have no idea how long we sit together or what we talk about. But each time Rob's lungs stop functioning, we all panic, expecting this to be the end. He fools us time and time again. Then his eyes open!

I can't believe it. This is the miracle I've been waiting for! He's coming back from the edge of death! We talk to him eagerly, but he doesn't answer. His eyes don't appear to register anything—they stare straight ahead. I call Charlotte.

"This is typical," she says. "He is not alert. He is not coming back. His body is nearly fully shut down now, and what happened is only a muscular reaction. You can close his eyelids."

Speight reaches forward and lowers Rob's lids. They pop open again and again. "Come on, Mulloy," he says, trying to be lighthearted. "Don't be a pain in the butt." The scene gives us a moment of dark comic relief. Rob's last joke.

But it's enough to give us a shred of irrational hope. Maybe he will come back and be well. We talk to Rob. I wonder if he can hear. A thousand thoughts surge through my brain. We wait for him to open his eyes again. We wait for his breath to steady. We wait … for nothing.

Time becomes nonexistent. I tell Angel about the lock. She stares at me, her eyes wide. She climbs onto the bed, curls up next to Rob and holds him tight, her face buried in his neck. She doesn't talk or move for a long time. Then she sits up. "I'm ready. But I want the three of us to do it together."

Since the lock is closest to me, I open it. Tears pour down my face.

"Okay. I'll start." A thought crashes through my head—I brought him into the world thirty-five years ago. Now I'm about to help him leave. I put my shaking finger on the button. Angel puts hers on top of mine. Ric covers ours with his. And we push together for I don't know how long.

Angel crumples onto Rob, her body cemented against his, her arms in a death grip around him.

Ric and I hold Rob's hands. And each other's.

The room is silent except for Rob's rattling breath, which slows, and slows ... and stops.

CHAPTER 43

A Mournful Cry

March 4, 2004   Studio City, California

I'M LYING ON THE Boltin's couch. I'm hot, yet I'm chilled and shaking. Someone must have tucked a blanket around me, because I'm wrapped suffocatingly tight like a burrito. How did I get here? Have I been dreaming? Everything is surreal and slow, like I'm underwater. Where is everyone?

Then I remember.

A hole the size of Kansas rips my heart apart. An inhuman wail comes from somewhere deep inside me.

Charlotte walks quietly into the room, sits next to me, and takes my hand. When did she get here? "I'm so sorry," she says with tears in her eyes. We sit without talking.

"Is there anything you want from the apartment?" she finally asks. "I'm going over there now."

"No." I can't imagine there is anything I could ever want again, other than bringing my son back to life.

"Wait. Yes. There is something you can get for me. Next to Rob is a raggedy stuffed animal, an owl, with only one orange leg and a missing eye. Ric and I gave it to him on his first birthday. He kept it all these years. He asked for it yesterday before he lapsed into a coma."

Charlotte returns with Owl. I wrap my arms around it and hold it close to my heart, as if I am holding my son and not this tattered lump.

"Do you want to see Rob before the undertakers get here?" she asks.

"Undertakers? Oh, god. No. No, I want to remember him alive."

She takes a step toward the door.

"Wait. Yes. I want to see him."

She holds me steady as we walk to the apartment. "I want you to be prepared because physical changes are already taking place. When his heart stopped ..." The reality of his heart no longer beating smacks me hard. I know he is dead, but somehow the mental image of his heart stopping crushes me.

He is still, peaceful, beautiful. His struggle is over. The Rob Mulloy we know and love is gone. The color has drained from most of his face, leaving it chalky white. Only half of his upper lip still has a tinge of pink. I caress his face. It's cool. The warmth of his life is no longer there.

Rob, where are you? Where did you go?

I wonder if his spirit is still in this room. I wonder if he is standing next to me, trying to tell me it's okay, and now he is free. I wonder if there is any reality to the concept of spirit. I want it to be true, so I hold on to it.

"Are you ready?" Charlotte puts her arm around me and guides me back to the Boltin's. It's dark outside, and it's cold.

I have a vague memory of two men in the courtyard wearing black suits and hats. I think I hear Charlotte say, "They have come for the body."

Sometime in the middle of the night, someone takes me back to Rob and Angel's apartment so I can get some sleep. I'm shocked when I walk in. The hospital bed is gone, the furniture is back in place, all the paraphernalia of death and dying is gone. I wonder if I am dreaming. I fall into my bed and sleep fitfully. Angel stays at the Boltin's for the night. I am alone.

A wretched howling noise awakens me in the night. It scares the hell out of me. What is it? I jump out of bed and run to the living room, shaking. There is DeNiro, Rob's kitty, standing at the front door, yowling. It's a haunting and mournful cry. He doesn't stop. I try to comfort him, but he continues to yowl. I sit down next to him, pull him close, and we cry together.

***

Someone is knocking. What time is it? I throw on a robe and start back to where I left DeNiro in the wee hours. Right outside my bedroom door, I see one of Rob's white socks lying on the carpet. It wasn't there last night. What's it doing here? I pick it up and tuck it into my pocket. The knocking continues.

"Hi, is Angel here?" a young man asks. A woman carrying a black medical-type bag stands next to him. "I'm the vet, and this is my assistant. We have an appointment at nine o'clock."

"Come in. Angel is not here. Do you need her? She's not feeling well this morning." I try to sound normal.

"It would be nice if she were here to tell me if there have been any problems with the cats over the past year. But I can do their physicals, and she and I can connect later."

I watch at a distance as the two of them carry on with muscle testing the cats. It's an alternative medical technique using muscle strength or weakness to indicate wellness or illness.

I've experienced it myself, but never imagined it could work with animals.

"DeNiro seems stressed. Has anything happened to him?"

"Well, uh, yes." I try unsuccessfully to maintain some control. "Rob died last night. Here in the apartment."

He blinks a few times. "Rob died? Here? You mean last night? It just happened last night?" He looks around the room.

"Yes."

"Oh, no. I'm so sorry. I can come back."

"No, I think as long as you are here, it will be helpful to have this done. I think the kitties need some TLC right now." I tell him about DeNiro howling at the door and how the Peewoos watched over Rob. He seems intrigued with their devotion and concerned about their trauma. The vet's assistant hands me packets of something organic to ease the kitties' stress. They finish up and leave.

I pull Rob's sock out of my pocket. My mind wants its arrival at my door to be supernatural. It wants Rob's spirit to have dropped it there to tell me he's nearby, even though I know it was DeNiro that put it there. I hold it close, trying to connect.

CHAPTER 44

Arrangements

March 5, 2004   Los Angeles, California

I FEEL HOLLOW INSIDE. Everything I see has a pea soup fog around it that dulls its vibrancy and movement. When someone speaks to me, the fog muffles their words, and my hearing is time-delayed, as if I am watching a movie in which the actions and speech are out of sync.

The apartment is eerily quiet. Ric is at his hotel. The Core Four, minus one, are at the Boltin's, planning Rob's Celebration of Life service in Griffith Park according to his instructions—must be outdoors, must have fun, no one wears black, only jeans and tees, play Grateful Dead music.

Angel and I are together, but separate, each lost in our own thoughts. We are interrupted only when someone needs pictures for the giant photo collage boards, when someone brings food and encourages us to eat, or when someone asks me, "Did you know you have a white sock tucked into your waistband?" This gives me the opportunity to tell the sock-at-my-bedroom-door story, which makes me feel as if Rob is still here. Otherwise this amazing bunch of friends is taking charge of every detail from securing a special place in the park that Rob loved, to ordering chairs and flowers, to planning the big party afterwards.

Ric, Angel, and I go to the mortuary to discuss cremation with the undertaker. I hate everything about this process, especially those guys in the grey suits and ties who work in funeral sales, who, it seems clear to me, take advantage of the emotional states of their customers for their own gain.

"I'm so sorry for the loss of your loved one," one of the grey suits offers with an extended hand. I don't want to touch him, but I do, reluctantly and briefly. He ushers us into his somber-toned office and places himself behind a large, polished desk. We sit opposite him in cushy chairs and make arrangements for Rob's cremation. He guides us gently to the topic of urns, but I only hear fragments of what he says because I'm hyper-aware that somewhere in a very cold part of this warehouse-like building, Rob's body is lying in a plastic zipper bag, on a shelf. The vivid image my brain conjures up disturbs me deeply.

The grey suit puts the gentle but manipulative push on us. "I'm sure you'll feel comforted knowing Rob's final resting place will be in one of our premium urns, crafted from the finest bronze and buffed to bring out its natural luster." He places an elaborate sample in front of us. It is implied that we are to pick it up and admire it. No one does. "A dignified eternal memorial for your loved one that you can put on display in your homes and feel proud."

The overuse of "loved one," his demure yet exploitive manner, and this bronze abomination piss me off. The hard-bargaining former antique dealer in me, who has had many go-rounds with the toughest New York dealers, rises to the surface. "Are they included in the price of cremation?"

My non-emotional tone catches him off guard, but he recovers quickly. "Well, no, they are not."

"How much are they?"

We gasp together when he quotes, "Thirteen-hundred forty-nine dollars and ninety-five cents each." Everyone squirms. "But, if you want three, one for each of you, I can definitely work with you on the price."

"Is this all you have to offer? What about something more moderately priced?"

He produces additional samples. The prices are all still ridiculous, and the urns are ugly.

"You don't have anything in a gentler price range, say, under a hundred dollars?"

He stiffens a little, then reaches into a cabinet and pulls out a sectioned tray filled with small, but lovely urns. I spot several that are cloisonné, which has always been a favorite art form of mine. "What about those? How much are they?"

"Forty-five dollars."

I pull one out and hold it in my hands. "I like this one with the enameled fish. Rob was a swimmer and a Pisces. It's perfect." Angel selects one with white doves, Ric chooses a contemporary design, and together we pick a nature scene for Shannon. Ric signs the paperwork and hands over a credit card. Cremation will be in two days.

This setting reminds me of when my brother-in-law died, and my sister and I went to the funeral home to make arrangements. The salesman ushered us into a room filled with ornate open caskets on display in every color and style. He guided my sister from box to box, each with its own glorified description—"the Lincoln model, eighteen-gauge steel, continuous weld construction so nothing can penetrate, luxurious tufted-velvet interior that comes in a variety of colors to compliment the highly polished exterior, which come in a variety of tasteful hues. Notice the artfully crafted gold handles. And there is a fully insured product warranty."

Warranty? Who will ever know if something goes wrong? It was the quote in the thousands that cleared my head and brought me to my senses. I could tell my sister was struggling between eternal-rest-in-style guilt and her budget.

"What about this one?" I asked, standing in front of a beautiful oak casket. It was simple, nothing like the Vegas abominations in the rest of the room. "Charlie loved simplicity in design, and he loved natural wood. He was always chopping down dead trees and cutting huge piles of firewood. Remember when he burned his eyebrows off making a bonfire?" Our laugh broke the tension. "This grain in this wood is beautiful. I think he would like this one." The salesman quoted a reasonable price. She agreed, much to his chagrin, and we moved on.

Another memory surfaces. I recall my dad telling me how, as a child, cremation was a process the entire family would view. "It was 1915, I was only six years old," he began. "We were in a passageway with big windows on one side. Inside were metal tracks that went through some big flames. Suddenly a wooden box, with Uncle Harry's body lying in it, came out of a door, moved along the tracks, and stopped in the middle of the fire. As the box became engulfed in flames and Uncle Harry began to burn, he suddenly sat straight up in the middle of the fire! Oh man! Everybody started to scream. The undertaker said it was a natural thing, the muscles were contracting in the heat. But I'll tell ya, Ellyn, that was the scariest thing that ever happened to me. I'll never forget it."

I try to shake this memory from my head and not apply it to what will happen to my son's body in two days. The grey suit tells us it's a dignified process. He hands Ric a receipt. "We will take very good care of your loved one. You needn't worry about a thing. We will fill the urns respectfully and mail them with the remainder of the ashes to Angel within the week."

CHAPTER 45

Farewell

March 7, 2004   Griffith Park, Los Angeles, California

ROWS OF WHITE CHAIRS stand out sharply against the verdant beauty of Griffith Park. They fill quickly as people arrive for Rob's Celebration of Life. Some guests stand, some spread blankets on the grass, the rest sit quietly. A huge poster of Rob with his awesome smile watches over everyone. Grateful Dead music fills the air. Angel, Ric, and I take our places in the front row alongside Shannon and Grandma Mulloy, who flew in late last night. Boltin is fiddling with a portable microphone and speaker at the dais. A loud "Test, test" interrupts Jerry Garcia, followed by empty silence.

The Core Three take the stage, a grassy niche among the trees, surrounded by pots of cheery daisies provided by the mother of another friend. These men, who were at Rob's side in full caregiving capacity over the past ten months, tell endearing and funny stories that move the audience from laughter to tears and back again. I am so overcome with emotion that I have trouble absorbing what they are saying. My daughter's hand, squeezing mine to near crushing, is the only sense of reality I have. Rich Speight brilliantly dramatizes a long, funny narrative that has something to do with Rob and a suitcase.

JT breaks down and can barely get through his homage, and Shannon reads a loving tribute to Rob from his dad and me.

The memorial ends. "What a Wonderful World" by Louis Armstrong plays at my request. Clumps of people surround the three photo collage boards. Fingers point to various pictures. A chorus of, "Oh! I remember this!" rings out with lots of bittersweet chatter.

I spot a familiar face in the crowd. It's Mauro, Rob's therapist. "I'm so pleased to see you. Thank you for coming. Rob would have loved knowing you are here."

"Rob was a remarkable young man. I am grateful to have spent time with him. If there's anything I can do to help you, or if you just need to talk, I'm here." He presses his business card into my hand. "Feel free to call."

By the time we get to Rich and Jaci's, the party is in full swing. The mood is happy, as Rob wanted it to be. I move from group to group. The endless Mulloy stories I hear and the laughter in the room lift me out of the horror of the past weeks. I find myself in a circle of his friends, giggling. In the den, a monitor plays a short comedy in a constant loop. The star is Rob. I join several others on the couch to watch.

An hour into the gathering, Grandma Mulloy is outside having a snit fit. "I don't understand how these people can laugh at a time like this. What's wrong with them?" An awkward silence ensues. She is exhausted, emotionally and physically, and needs to return to her hotel. We have only one car, and if Grandma Mulloy wants to leave, we all have to go. I'm extremely annoyed that she, a former actress herself, is upstaging this gathering, superseding my desire, my need to stay. We try to figure out a way for me to get back to Angel and Rob's apartment, but nothing works. Shannon gives me the "You know what Grandma is like when she gets into her actress mode" look. I passive aggressively take my time as I go back inside to say my goodbyes. A half hour later Shannon finds me, squeezes my hand, and walks me to the car.

CHAPTER 46

Sorting It Out

March 20, 2004   Studio City, California

ANGEL'S ON A TEAR, sorting through Rob's things, cleaning out closets, aiming for a fresh start on her life.

I leave for an appointment with Mauro, taking him up on his offer to help. I was so pleased to see him at Rob's Celebration of Life.

It seems odd to be here at a counseling session without Rob. But then everything, every minute of every day seems odd without Rob. I sit in the middle of the couch, drop my purse and keys on the cushion next to me, cross my legs and wonder where to begin.

"That's exactly where Rob sat. And he would drop his wallet and keys in the same place. I notice the two of you have similar facial expressions and similar gestures. I could pick you two out in a crowd as mother and son."

"I take that as a real compliment. Thank you." I pull out one of Rob's head shots from a folder I brought and give it to Mauro. He looks at it with tears in his eyes. "Thank you for this. It means a lot. Rob was a very special young man."

He picks up a book and reads to me from a chapter entitled, "What Makes A Good Death?" He looks at me. "You did all these for him. You did everything you possibly could—he died in a comfortable place with people he loved, he knew he was loved, you all worked out any lingering issues, and friends and family were there to help." These are powerful words for me to hear. No wonder Rob loved working with this man. Throughout the next hour we talk in depth, exchange Rob stories, and a tiny fragment of me begins to heal.

On the way back to the apartment, I think about how Rob held on to his child-self. He had an impishness about him that inspired fun. On their bedroom wall hangs a print of Kermit the Frog, his childhood favorite and, apparently, an adult favorite as well. My plan is to take it back to Massachusetts with me, as a symbol of his Muppetty outlook on life. I know Angel is eager to replace it with something more to her liking. But when I arrive, the print is gone.

"Where's Kermit?" I ask Angel.

"I took him and several other pictures down to the laundry room, where people in the complex share stuff they no longer want."

I fly down the stairs and find the stack of framed prints. Apparently, there is another Kermit lover in the building because he is gone. I'm devastated and feel as if another piece of my son has been taken from me.

Angel asks me to go through the closets with her and take anything I want. I touch the empty sleeve of his USC swimming jacket, aware of the tremendous energy that once filled it and the pride he had in earning his place on the team. "I'd like to have this," I whisper. I really want everything in the closet, but I select a USC tee shirt and another one of his favorites, Calvin and Hobbs. I put a Harpoon Brewery cap on my head. A Fannie Mae candy box marked "Ephemera" in Rob's handwriting catches my eye. It's filled with letters from his grandmother and from me. I cry with each item of his that I touch and clutch it to my heart. I fill another box with his swim medals, props from plays, and handwritten lyrics from his favorite Grateful Dead songs, song lyrics he had composed at boyhood summer camp, and several he recorded and shopped to agents.

The doorbell rings. Packages from friends have been arriving daily, thoughtful gifts to help ease the pain—bath salts and lotions, books, endless amounts of food. Today's package has no return address, no indicators of any kind to advertise its sender. It's heavy and big. Angel and I sit on the couch. She slices through the tape on the top with a box cutter and opens the flaps. There is a plastic bag filled with something we can't identify. She pulls it out, and a surge of white powder spills over her black pants, covers my shoes, and piles up on the carpet. Apparently, the blade sliced through the plastic bag.

"What the heck is this stuff? And who is it from? There's no card." She tries to dust it off her clothes. It sticks to her hands.

We look in the box again and see four cloisonné urns. Then it hits us. These are Rob's ashes.

Angel's face registers horror. "Oh, my god!"

We sit on the couch silently staring at the ashes. Then I burst out laughing. "This is ridiculous. Here's Rob making his comedic mark one last time, covering us in his ashes, making his presence known in a dramatic way! Think about it, Angel. He would have loved this."

We sit there and laugh through our tears while we scoop up what we can with our hands. I rub my powdery fingers together, noting how soft he feels. This is my son's body.

CHAPTER 47

Buzz Buzz

March 23, 2004   San Diego, California

I KEPT BUSY WHILE in LA, but my role there is finished. Angel needs to get her life sorted out on her own, but I'm not ready to go home yet, not ready to be alone in my house. So, I go to San Diego, to Ginger's house.

Separating myself from Rob's home, his wife, their kitties, and all the turmoil of his illness and death leave me lost and feeling the finality of it all. I kept myself somewhat together emotionally as long as I needed to, but now that the activity is over, and I've left LA, I'm flattened out and despondent. Yesterday I spent the entire day in a chair reading, thinking, remembering with little energy for anything else. Today I made myself get up and go out with Ginger to find tile for her bathroom. Tomorrow I'll try to add a little more activity, but mainly I need rest.

The phone rings. It's my sister. "I have a message for you."

"Oh? Who's it from?"

"Rob."

I stop breathing. My heart races. "Rob?"

Linda continues, excited. "I was relaxing this morning when suddenly I had a vision. I 'saw' Dad (who died in 1991) in front of me. Rob was standing to his side, looking very healthy, smiling that big Rob smile. He told me to tell you, 'Mr. Bumblebee, buzz buzz.' I don't know what that means, but that's what he told me to tell you."

"You saw Rob! He looked healthy? He was smiling? He was with Dad? Really? Really? He said that?" I'm alive with excitement. "And, by the way, it's 'Buzz buzz, Mr. Bumblebee!'"

"What does that mean?" she asked.

"I never told you the story?"

"No."

"Are you SURE I never told you the story?" I wanted to make certain this was real and not Linda's imagination re-creating what she already knew.

"NO! Now tell me the story!"

"It was 1992. Rob was home from college for spring break and we went to play golf. As we got out of the car in the golf course parking lot, we stopped for a minute to talk, facing each other. We heard a loud buzz, then the largest bumble bee I had ever seen zoomed right between our faces. We watched it zigzag away, then we looked at each other. At exactly the same time, both Rob and I chimed out in sing-songy voices, 'Buzz BUZZ, Mr. Bumblebee!'

"We stared at each other, our mouths agape, amazed we would each say such a weird thing at the same time. And with the same sing-songy intonation! Then Rob said, 'I always thought I was unique and even kind of eccentric, but now I know I'm just my mother.'

"I loved hearing that, and I laughed. He looked freaked out.

"That's the story, but there's more. Right before he died, I said to Rob, 'When you get to the other side, please, please find a way to let me know you're okay.'

"So, this bumblebee experience was something he and I shared. It was exclusively ours alone. This must be his way of letting me know he's okay. How awesome! Thank you."

I hang up the phone and sit quietly, gratefully. I wonder about the "other side" and where it is, what it is, and what's it like for him to be there.

CHAPTER 48

More Change

March 25, 2004   San Diego, California

I KNEW LAST OCTOBER this moment was coming, but compared to what's been going on with Rob, this event is trivial, and I relegated it to the back of my mind. The company that employs me will be officially acquired next week, and my job as Director of Work/Life will be gone, along with the jobs of 499 others in Human Resources and one thousand more employees throughout our many offices. This is typical in an acquisition. The buyer's employees are the ones who survive. The buyee's employees are out the door.

I'm already fractured inside from grief and loss and refuse to put up with any harassment. This means I refuse to have anything to do with my unpleasant manager. So, I call Jerry, the HR guy for HR.

"Ellyn. How nice to hear your voice. I'm so sorry to hear about your son. What a terrible loss. How are you doing? Where are you?"

"Thanks, Jerry. I'm San Diego now with friends. Everything in LA is finished. Rob's memorial service is over, and Angel and I got things organized at their home. I'm going to Oregon in a few days to spend some time with my brother and his family. I'll be home to Annisquam on April 10.

"I got an email a while ago about April 1 as our last day of work and want to know what I have to do. Do I need to be there?"

"Not at all. You just stay there and take good care of yourself. Everything is complete, and it's all paperwork at this point. I'll overnight your package. You sign a couple forms, and it's all done. I know you don't want to deal with your manager. I understand that completely. It's not a problem. I'll be your contact from now on. Call me anytime about anything. We're all thinking about you and wish you peace and healing."

"You're the best, Jerry. Thank you so much."

I scribble my name on the layoff papers and overnight them back to Jerry. This timing couldn't be better. The idea of going back to work right now is abhorrent to me. I'm not sleeping, not eating, not functioning very well. I've lost twelve pounds from stress. My body is a vacant shell. I know I'm moving around, and I'm talking, but there is little connection with my sense of self, which is out there somewhere, wandering in a dense fog, trying to make sense of life. And of death.

· PART III ·

OREGON

CHAPTER 49

Russell

April 1, 2004   Portland, Oregon

"COME TO MY HOUSE," my brother said over the phone. "You're exhausted and need some rest. Let Mary, RT, and me take care of you."

He's right. I'm so deeply sad, so confused and disoriented that I don't have the energy or even the desire to take care of myself. I accept his invitation. On the flight, I pull out the journal I kept when we reconnected two years ago and read it as a distraction. The parts about nature are soothing, but the other topics are heavy, and unbeknownst to Russell and me, carry a foreboding.

—

September 20, 2002   Portland, Oregon

Russell took me up into the Cascades today, along the Clackamas River. What utter majesty in the old-growth trees, the basalt cliffs, the shallow end-of-summer river splashing over smooth stones while winding its way down the mountain. We picked our way along the rocky shore, then hopped from stepping-stone to stepping-stone out to the middle of the river where we settled down on a dry flat boulder.

He lifted his shirt, pulled out a gun he had tucked into the back of his jeans, and laid it next to him on the rock.

"I didn't know you had that back there," I said, surprised. "Aren't you afraid you'll shoot yourself in the butt?" I chuckled.

"Ha! It won't happen. The safety is on."

"Why do you carry a gun? It kinda freaks me out."

"Never go into the mountains without a gun. We're in the wild, and we're isolated out here. There's no telling what could happen. Some crazy guy or hungry wild animal could come walking out of the woods at any time. You don't want to be in the wrong place at the wrong time without protection."

I choose my next words carefully, not wanting to cause a rift. "I understand that. But I have to say, Russ, because of so many accidental shootings in homes across the country, I don't like the idea of people having guns in their houses. But what you just said sheds a new light on the subject for me. A weapon in a wilderness environment makes sense. And that's probably why there's such a controversy—different situations call for different actions. One law does not cover them all."

He looked at me, listening.

"There's a billboard along the Mass Turnpike in Boston," I continued. "It's huge, 250 feet long, and it's filled with photos of kids who have been killed by handguns. This is what bothers me about guns in the home. Accidents happen."

"Parents need to teach their kids gun safety. I taught RT from the time he was little."

"But accidents still happen," I offered one last time.

"Yeah, they do. And that's a terrible thing."

I watched a stick work loose from a logjam and float down the river. Then I asked him, "Why do you think we didn't get along as kids?"

He answered immediately. "That's easy. You thought you were better than the rest of us."

I stopped cold. I wanted to react and defend myself, but I took time to think before I responded. "I've grown a lot over the years," I told him.

"I can see that just in the little time we've been together."

"I'm more grounded, more focused."

"It's about time."

I prickled a little. I worked hard to become my own person, which involved breaking away from my family to find my own place in the world, a place that was me, in which I could unfold my Ellyn petals and blossom.

"I didn't intend to be judgmental," I said. "I only wanted more out of my life than I had growing up. I wanted to go to college so I could get a job that was meaningful. And I didn't want to worry about money all the time like mom and dad. It took a while to find my place, and I finally have. I learned along the way to not judge my family or those who want something different. I'm sorry if I hurt you."

"Thank you for that. You were the smartest one. It was right for you to go to college. I hated school."

"Each of us kids is smart in our own way. I love creativity, literature and the arts. Linda is amazing with numbers and is almost a master gardener. You're talented with your hands and can figure out complicated things. Look at the beautiful kitchen and living room you built by yourself, and you're not even a carpenter. You intuitively know how to do that. I don't and never will."

"Well, that's true. There were many times at work when the giant presses broke down and no one could figure out what was wrong. Management always called me because I was the only one in the company who could see what the problem was and fix it."

"That's what I'm talking about. There are different kinds of smart. Everyone has their own special skills, their own way of excelling in the world. One way is not better than another. I'm not better than you or anyone else, just different."

Years of misunderstanding washed away downstream.

We talked for at least an hour, maybe more, about our parents, our kids, and how our differing beliefs shaped our lives. Then we sat in silence listening to the music of the river as it spilled over the rocks.

"We're gonna meet Mary and some friends at the Beaver Crick Saloon tonight. We'd better get going."

"Did you say 'crick'?"

"Creeeek to you Easterners."

We laughed.

The Saloon was lively with locals in various stages of alcohol-induced bliss. We found Mary and their gang at a table near the bar. After a beer or two and a lot of conversation and laughter, Russ leaned close to me. "Why don't you move here?" he asked. "Get yourself out of that damn rat race you're in. Come out here and relax a little."

Life here appears to be easier. Not sure if this is true or just the apparent perfection of someplace new. I compare how laid back and happy Russ is and how stressed I am. In Oregon, the cost of living and the pace are dramatically different. If I left my Boston job and sold my house, I could pay cash for a similar home here, then work at an easier pace to support myself. But, would I choose a life of calm and simplicity, more like my brother's, over my more complicated life? Not likely.

My home in Annisquam is perched on a forested hill overlooking the Jones River and the Atlantic Ocean, a serene environment. It's as breath-taking as the Cascades, but in different ways. The Atlantic has a personality that changes constantly—from a dangerous temptress smashing against the granite shoreline, the spindrift dancing above the jagged rocks, to a sweet damsel spilling softly over the sandy beaches, tickling your toes. I love the tide's ebb and flow, a rhythm that plays out subtly. If I am still, I can sense from a primitive place within the exact moment when the tide changes. It's an ethereal experience that never fails to link me with the interconnectedness of all living things. I have tranquility in my Massachusetts life—it's all around me in Mother Nature. I don't need a geographic move to find serenity. All I have to do is sit quietly and let it in.

Russ and I both have a deep religious appreciation for nature, instilled in us by our dad. The forest is our church, the trees our minister, and the perfect harmony and balance of all things in nature is our bible. We need nothing more. Amen.

"Moving here would be nice," I said to Russ, "but I'll stay where I am. Shannon lives nearby, which is great.

But, if I relocated, it would be Southern California to get out of the wretched winters. And Rob lives there."

—

September 21, 2002

Mary stayed home today while Russ and I drove to the coast. "You two need more time together," she said.

The drive to the coast was all about talking. Russ opened up about Vietnam. I felt honored he trusted me enough to speak freely about war horrors he buried deep inside almost forty years ago. Horrors that cause him to isolate from other people and perhaps from me. "I never told this to anybody," he began tentatively. He gripped the steering wheel and stared straight ahead. His knuckles turned white, and his lips got tight as if they were trying to hold the words in.

"The Army told us never to tell anyone anything about the shit they made us do. And I never have." He paused, pushed his left hand over his mouth, his thumb sinking into his cheek. He looked out the side window, then back to the road ahead.

"The terror is still there though. It's still inside me." He started to choke. His blue eyes darkened, and tears fell down his face as he described the gruesome details of how so many of his buddies lost their lives. "Ellyn, I was standing near our tent one night talking with my buddy, John. We lit our cigarettes. A sniper in the jungle must have seen the light and fired. I heard the crack of the gunshot, and then John's head exploded. He fell into me. Dead. We were both covered in his blood. How do you live with the memory of something like that?"

He took a breath and continued—now that he started, it was as if he couldn't stop.

"Every day I woke up thinking this could be my last day alive. I knew Charlie was out there somewhere and wanted me dead.

"About ten o'clock one night—it was stinking hot with humidity that never stopped day after day. Wretched humidity. None of us guys ever had dry socks, and that sucked, but that's neither here nor there. Anyway, my buddy and I were driving to the place we always dumped the garbage. Ha! Garbage duty, it was lousy work, but it was better than some of the jobs the other guys had to do.

"We came to the fork in the road where I usually turned right to unload the truck in a clearing about 200 yards down the road. That fuckin' jungle on both sides of us was so damn thick I couldn't see more than a few inches into it. There could be Viet Cong standing in there, and you'd never even see them. But I'll tell ya, Ellyn, that Agent Orange shit they used to defoliate was evil. I'm still having breathing problems from it, and the VA says there's nothing they can do about it.

"Anyway, I was grinding the gears of the truck into low so we wouldn't get stuck in those damn mud ruts when, oh man, all of a sudden I became paralyzed with fear. This wasn't the usual fear that haunted all of us guys every second of every day. This was something else, something much stronger—a feeling came over me that was so clear it was almost alive. I paid attention and stopped the truck. I don't know what it was. I couldn't describe it, but I knew beyond a doubt that if I turned right down the usual road, I would die.

"I sat there frozen for a while, then turned left to find a new dumping place. I guess my face turned white because my buddy Ray said, 'What's goin' on Russ? Are you all right?' I radioed camp and told them what happened. They listened and sent some guys to check it out. Sure enough, those damn Viet Cong must have been watching us, knew our regular route, and planted a booby trap in the road—a fuckin' land mine that would have blown Ray and me to bits. I almost bought it that day. I guess it wasn't my time."

Russ took a deep breath.

"But that wasn't the worst. I had a secret clearance to get information from the Viet Cong we captured. The Army instructed our guys to take them up in a helicopter with an interpreter and hold guns to their heads. If they wouldn't talk, we'd shove one guy out the door and watch him fall to his death. The other guy always panicked and talked. God, Ellyn, after he gave us what we wanted, we were ordered to shove him out the door too. Then we'd go back to the print trailer and make maps that directed the next attack.

"I can't believe we did that shit. It haunts me. I still have nightmares to this day and wake up screaming."

Telling me the stories took Russ right back emotionally and physically to Da Nang. His face drained of all color, and he shook as he relived the experiences. Overcome, he pulled the car over to the side of the road. "I need a minute. I don't want to have an accident. That fuckin' Nam has me all screwed up—and it's been almost 40 years."

All I could do was put my hand gently on his shoulder and wait quietly while he pulled himself together. I'll never fully grasp the terror he experienced there, nor the PTSD that plagues him still.

I can't help but think about that very clear feeling that gripped him while driving the garbage truck, the one that told him not to turn right, the one that saved him from being blown to bits by a land mine. Could it be the same voice that told me to come to Oregon and reconnect with my brother?

—

September 22, 2002   Portland, Oregon

RT lives at home with my brother and Mary. He's sensitive like his dad, has a passion for maximizing life's experiences, oozes artistic creativity, and is consumed by a whole lot of wanderlust. Off at a Renaissance Faire somewhere in Virginia with his tribe of friends, he won't be back until after I leave, which is too bad because the last time I saw him was at my parent's fiftieth wedding anniversary. He was eleven.

He hasn't found a career yet that holds his interest. He talked with his dad last month about signing up for the Air Force Reserve. Russell is close to his son ("He's my best friend.") and had a visceral reaction to this based on his own Vietnam War experience. "No way I'll support this hair-brained idea!"

Russell told me he called the recruiter who was after RT. "Listen. Russell Troy is my only son, my only child. I will not allow him to risk his life in another bullshit war. Have you ever felt the fear of knowing someone wants you dead, and they're out there hunting you? Have you ever been talking to your buddy when his head is blown apart by a sniper's bullet? Don't take my son."

He said the recruiter stumbled over his words at first. "Ah. Well. No. I appreciate what you say, Sir. But he is of age, and it is his decision. Sir."

Russell asked RT why he wanted to sign up.

"My best friend Joe was killed in Afghanistan. I feel I have to right this wrong, Dad. I owe it to him to do my part and take over for him."

Russell told me he knew then and there that RT was going, and there was nothing he could do about it. And with the Iraq War on the Bush administration's horizon, I expect a phone call soon from Russell telling me RT is in uniform.

The captain's voice crackles over the PA, bringing me back to the present. "That's Crater Lake on the right side of the aircraft, folks. The deepest lake in the US." From the airplane window, I spot a large body of intensely blue water with an island in the middle that looks familiar. I remember a sepia-tone photograph I saw as a child—my mom sitting on a huge rock overlooking a body of water in the distance with an island in the middle. Her legs folded to one side, her torso facing away from the camera toward the lake. "That's me at Crater Lake in Oregon," Mom told me each time I saw the picture. "It was a sad time. Dad took me there after we lost Richard." Richard was my parent's first child who died when he was five days old.

What a weird twist of fate. Here I am, looking at Crater Lake, just as my mom did sixty years ago, experiencing the same debilitating grief as she did back then. I'm startled by the coincidence.

Then another memory from almost two-and-a-half years ago seeps in. That voice, or whatever it was, telling me, "It's time to rekindle your relationship with your brother." Where did that come from? What is intuition anyway? Is there a larger body of knowledge out there that guides us to what we need to do, or where we need to go? Are there higher beings, spirits, angels, or friends and relatives who have passed who look out for us from the other side?

Suddenly, I realize the deeper intention in the message—that someone or something transcendent knew Rob was going to die, and I would need my brother for support. Goose bumps rise on my arms, and I sit in awe as I consider this. But wait, why my brother and not my sister? I was closer to her at the time. The question goes as quickly as it came. It's all too overwhelming, and we just landed in Portland.

CHAPTER 50

Healing Again

April 1, 2004   Portland, Oregon

DÉJÀ VU GRIPS ME as I walk through the Portland airport. My brother is standing at the baggage carousel, waiting for me, the same scenario as two years ago. Only this time neither one of us is smiling. My control disintegrates when he throws his arms around me and holds me tight.

"My darling little sister. This is the worst thing ever. But you're here now, and Mary, RT and I are going to take care of you."

At the house Mary leads me to the guest room where she embraces me. RT steps into the room and immediately joins the hug. "Auntie Ellyn," he whispers, emotion cracking his voice. "I'm so sorry." I feel an instant familiar connection with him. He's only a couple years younger than Rob, he's filled with energy, and—he's alive.

I don't remember eating dinner, just falling into bed and conking out until sunrise, when I hear a knock on my door. It's RT. "Are you up for an adventure after breakfast?"

A distraction. Thank goodness. "Sounds great. What do you have in mind?"

"Get dressed, wear sturdy shoes, grab your swimsuit and a towel. I have a surprise for you."

He loads our gear into his truck, tucks a gun into his boot, and we head toward the mountains after stopping at a convenience store for a couple Red Bulls. He downs his first in a few gulps.

RT relaxes into the driver's seat, steering with his left arm, his right free to adjust the radio to an oldies station, which I assume is for my benefit. He rolls his shirt sleeve up, and I can see ink on his left arm. "That's an unusual star tattoo on your forearm," I say. "Tell me about it."

"It's an exact copy of the one my buddy Joe had on his arm. He died in Afghanistan six months ago. I joined the Air Force Reserve because I didn't want his death to be in vain. Looks like my unit will be shipped over there in the fall."

Oh my god, I think, but don't say.

Our conversation covers a variety of topics from how happy he is with his new profession as a pharmacist, to the heinous murders committed by a new extremist group called the Islamic State of Iraq and Syria, known as ISIS. Two hours slip by. RT slows the truck down and points out a log jam of giant trees uprooted by a raging river flood last spring. We stop on the bridge where I take his picture—the river with the tangle of trees in the background, his tattooed arm visible in the foreground.

We arrive at a parking lot, a dirt clearing among the massive Douglas firs, which loom 250 feet above us in Mount Hood National Forest. Two cars, dwarfed by their surroundings, wait patiently for their owners. A trail disappears into the sun-dappled darkness. RT grabs our bags, slings them over his shoulder, and off we go. This beautiful hike must be the surprise.

We're quiet as we walk along the narrow path, silenced by the magnificence of these towering pines. My thoughts go deep. My emotions bubble up. RT hands me a Kleenex without turning around and without a word, recognizing my need for privacy.

We hike for an hour. The forest is endless. Along the path is a monstrous felled tree, its center hollowed out. I'm humbled as I step inside and stand up straight inside the core of this colossus. RT snaps my picture, then guides me fifty feet ahead.

"Here it is," he announces with a smile. I'm stunned. In the middle of nowhere is a rough pine plank structure about forty feet by twenty feet with no roof, and walls that are only frames, so whoever is inside can still be outside.

In front of this "building" is a black rubber hose that comes out of the ground, goes to a wooden sluiceway that runs along a pine wall, and then stops. "What is this?" I ask.

"This is Bagby Hot Springs. That hose taps into a huge underground body of hot water. Let me show you where it goes."

We step inside the structure. It's a rustic spa! Three hollowed out tree trunks, like primitive dugout canoes, line the wall on the other side of the sluiceway. Each is wide enough for one person and long enough for two. The insides feel silky smooth to the touch. A round wooden tub that looks like a giant wine barrel sits in one corner. Four people are mellow in the hot spring water, high, I suspect as I sniff the air.

"There are changing rooms in that corner where you can get into your swimsuit. It's okay to leave your clothes there. Which log do you like? I'll fill it while you change."

"How do you fill it?"

He shows me an exquisite arrangement, everything made of wood from the forest, no unnatural materials except for hoses. He slides a small door up and turns a wooden spigot, which releases hot water from the sluiceway. It gushes into a downspout and into the log bathtub.

"Holy cow! That's awesome! But it's boiling hot!"

"There's another hose at the other end of the tub that draws water from the river we crossed a while back, the one with the logjam. It's ice cold, and it's safe because it's an A river, no pollution, no bacteria. Why don't you control the cold water, so we get the right temperature mix."

The next hour we soak in our log and talk. RT's surprise surpasses anything I ever could have imagined.

But we're not finished. Back in the truck, we drive eighty-three miles back to Portland, where RT takes me to his favorite Asian restaurant for dinner. The waitress greets him with a hug and brings warm sake, which she pours into two small natural bamboo cups. "These cups are so cool! They're made from real bamboo reeds! I love them!"

We feast, then RT takes me to the International Rose Test Garden. "This was set up in 1917, during World War I, to preserve the European roses they thought might be decimated by the bombings. It's a popular spot. I thought you might like it."

By the time we get home, I'm charmed and oh-so-grateful for this amazing time with RT, my thoughtful nephew, who cleverly took me away from my grief for a day. Russ and Mary want to hear all about our adventure, and as I talk, RT excuses himself, only to return later with another gift for me. I rip open the tissue paper wrap and find a set of sake cups and a teapot, just like the ones in the restaurant. "I had some bamboo in the workshop and made these. I wanted to give you something to remember this day by."

Little did I know how much this gift, and this day, would mean to me come November.

April 3, 2004   Snake River, Eastern Oregon

RUSSELL DECIDES THE BEST thing for the two of us is to go fishing—the antidote to pain for all the males in my family. We make the eight-hour drive to the Snake River wilderness, the natural border between Oregon and Idaho.

"Here we are in paradise," he says as he pulls his truck off the highway and onto a narrow dirt road carved into the rolling green mountains on one side, and a thirty-foot drop into the river on the other. Russ visibly relaxes. An easy countenance replaces his highway-stressed face. Two miles in, we pass a sign that reads:

Welcome to Jack Gordon Oregon
Unincorporated
Elevation: 2096
Population: 2 or more

Hmmm. This gives a whole new meaning to remote, I think, as I gaze across the tranquil river to miles of desolate weather-worn mountains on the Idaho side. "I feel as if I'm on the moon."

"Yeah. It has that effect. There's nothing here other than a few crazy people who love to fish." Eighteen dusty miles later, I spot a smattering of homes, little dots nestled against six-thousand-foot mountains, each separated by acres of open land.

"This trailer on the left belongs to the Mayor of Fultonville. Real name's Bud, but we all call him The Mayor. Not sure why. He's not really a mayor, just another beer drinkin' buddy. Lives here year 'round.

"Over there is Jim B's fifth wheel that he leaves here during the summer. He was a big-time electrician before he retired. Made a bundle doing work in 'Nam and Saudi, but he doesn't spend it. He's so tight he squeaks, so we like to tease him about it. I bought this new truck last month, and told him I won it at the casino on a five-dollar bet. He just about turned green and nearly popped a gasket. But there's a heart of gold inside him. He wired this whole boat launch area by Mel's so we have electricity, and weekend friends can pull up their campers and plug in.

"Ha! There's Mel on his porch, waiting for us. He's turned his house, Melville, over to us for the four days we're here, and he's gonna stay in his fancy new RV. I think it's probably nicer than his house."

Mel, a fifty-something guy with a neatly trimmed white beard wears a red and black checked Pendleton zip-up jacket over a hooded grey sweatshirt, jeans and red-laced work boots. His constant companion, a small fluffy white dog named Gizmo, trots after him, looking like he should be the companion of a lunching lady and not a river dude. Mel approaches the car with a big smile as we come to a stop in his driveway. His blue eyes signal mischief. "Hey, you asshole, what took you so long to get here? Come on in, the beer is cold. Hey little sister, welcome to the river."

Russ hops out of the car. "Hey, you dipshit, you should have the beer open and ready for me right here in the driveway. I don't think I can make it all the way to the house. I've had a powerful thirst for the past eight hours." They both laugh and hug each other.

Mel embraces me. "You've been through a lot, little sister, but you're here now, and we're gonna take good care of you. You drink beer?"

April 4, 2004   Snake River, Eastern Oregon

I'M UP EARLY. I settle into a pine rocking chair on the front porch, and bask in the morning sun, alone with my thoughts. The quiet is so profound, it's almost loud. Idaho is dressed in soft green with a touch of grey-blue—scrubby sagebrush, punctuated with an occasional juniper. Snow clings to the mountain tops, but it's probably seventy degrees here in the sunshine. The river, no more than six hundred feet away, twinkles reflected sunshine into my eyes. It's calm, but I know there is life teeming below the surface.

Nature's tranquility pulls me in. I'm more peacefully observant of my feelings today than I was last night after dinner when turbulent grief got the better of me. I'm physically and emotionally exhausted. This is the first time I've felt protected and safe since Rob died. I'm with family now, with my big brother.

"I declare today a No Beer Day." Mel's hoarse whisper floats out the kitchen window along with the enticing aroma of freshly brewed coffee. He must have come in the back door, leaving me to my solitude. "A hearty breakfast will put us right, then watch out fish, we're comin' after you. Little sister, come on in here and put some bacon and eggs in your stomach. You'll need your strength today. We have fish to catch."

They both look like they've been trampled by a herd of elk, but my brother prepares a delicious meal as Mel refills coffee cups. I left them last night in the living room with their bottomless beers over an animated cribbage game. "You dirty dog!" were the last words I heard as I closed my door.

Russell kills the boat's motor over the hole he knows is filled with small-mouth bass and crappies. It's near the rocks on the Idaho side. I can't say which rocks, that's a family secret. He opens his tackle box and studies the vast array of colorful flies, lures and other paraphernalia. He picks a jig first, then changes his mind, takes out a purple rubber worm, and attaches it to my line. I'm all set to pull in tonight's dinner. Mel lands a nice bass on his first cast. Russell grumbles, then does the same. Together we bring in twenty-nine good-sized fish, eight of them mine. I'm both relaxed and distracted, my sadness temporarily set aside. Fishing is meditative while waiting, exciting while catching. Gizmo is unfazed by the activity and sleeps through it all.

We're back at Mel's fish cleaning area by the river's edge. Russ pulls a couple bass out of the stainless steel holding tank and lays them on the attached worktable to measure them. I'm busy getting the gear out of the boat. "Ellyn, come on over here. I want to take a picture of you with these two fourteen-inch beauties you caught," Russ says.

I hate touching fish. I did when I was a kid and my dad took me fishing, and I still do. After much cajoling, I reluctantly pick them up by their lips, and they are recorded. Russ goes to work with his filet knife. Mel brings his truck down so we can listen to some country tunes on the radio. He turns the volume up. We're all busy singing along, then Shania Twain comes on and in that soulful country voice sings, "It only hurts when I'm breathing. My heart only breaks when it's beating. My dreams only die when I'm dreaming. So, I hold my breath to forget."

Russ and Mel are busy cleaning fish and don't notice that I'm paralyzed with emotion, holding my breath to forget, my heart breaking while it's beating. I step behind the shed and try to get some control. It doesn't work.

I start to walk back to the house, my head down.

"Hey, where are you going?" Russ calls out.

"I'll be back later," I choke out, not turning around.

"Are you okay?"

"No."

"What happened? Ah, shit, it's the music. Mel, turn that damn thing off."

April 5, 2004   Snake River, Oregon

MY BROTHER LOADS ME onto the ATV and off we go for a grand tour up the mountain behind Mel's house. "Watch where you step. I shot a rattler at the back door last week. Seven rings on his tail!"

My gut pulls in sharply! My posture straightens into alert status. Growing up in Illinois, a snake meant that harmless wiggly thing with the yellow-green stripe down its side, a garter snake that ate rodents and bugs, a good creature to have around. But snakes with venom. Geez, I'm light-headed at the thought because I want to wander around through the brush and climb on the rocks when we reach the top of the mountain.

"What do you think of this view? Worth a million dollars. Nothing in any direction, except pure nature and a few crazy mountain people like me." Russ laughs his goofy laugh. "I love it here."

As I breathe in the clean air, my lungs do a happy dance. Boston's city air is unhealthy. Up here I can see for miles, no smog, no particulate matter, just clear unadulterated views. The tightness in my shoulders forgets why it's there and takes a little break.

We cruise carefully down the grassy mountainside, passing the remains of a tilting wooden shack and a tunnel, dug into the side of the mountain, both built by Chinese gold miners in the late Nineteenth Century. We cross the two-lane dirt road to the boat launch on the river. "The water's low right now. The dam downstream controls the water level, so the river up here has become a reservoir. The Snake starts in Wyoming, runs south through Jackson Hole, then it flows north up through Hell's Canyon and into the Columbia River in Washington. Used to be the salmon ran all the way down here, but now the hydroelectric dams stop them.

"Nearest big town is Boise, about an hour-and-a-half away. Nearest grocery store is in Ontario, sixty miles to the West. The five families who live here always check in with everybody else when they're going to town. If you forget an ingredient for a recipe, it's a real pain in the ass." Russ talks on and on, filling my imagination with details about the area and stories about the very interesting neighbors.

One is rather unique. Larry the gold miner.

"Ach, I'm not going to even bother describing him," Russ says. "You won't believe me anyway. Let's just go down there, and you can see for yourself. Be ready, you're in for somethin' real crazy."

"I'm pretty grubby. Should I change my clothes since we're visiting?"

Russell laughs. "Hop in the truck, Sis."

We pull up to what looks like a garbage dump sprawled in the crux of two mountains. Two rusty barrels, one with a grill grate on top, the other filled with burnable garbage, stand next to a charred wooden lamp post. A red gas can sits too close for comfort to the make-shift incinerator. Rags and wires spill out of a dozen white Home Depot-type buckets, which tilt hither and yon amid vast amounts of metal rubbish that I can't even describe. A faded and lumpy burnt orange recliner, its seat littered with more debris, sits in the dirt, much like you would see at curbside waiting to be picked up by the trash men, only this one isn't.

An ancient Chevy truck is parked near the road. It's multi-colored with replacement parts—peeling green paint over blue metal on the back, rusted out red on the doors, black on the roof. The bumper is gone, dangling red ropes that held it in place are all that remain. The front windshield has a large hole on the driver's side, with a twenty-by-twenty-inch piece of severely scratched and clouded plastic glued badly over it, leaving visibility at near zero. Russ kicks one of the balding tires. "Only four of the eight cylinders work. You can hear it chugging and banging as he drives down the road on his way to his mine on the mountain top. We keep telling him that one day it's gonna give out when he's up there, and he's gonna go sailing off into the blue. He just says, 'Bullshit.'"

Tangled ropes litter the ground. I nearly trip as I move in for a closer look at Larry's living quarters.

The Winnebago, or what appears to have been a Winnebago in better days, is wrapped by a large dark green tarp that covers the windshield, the leaky roof and most of the back, ending just above the propane tank. A spidery network of knotted red ropes dangles down from the roof and over the sides. The end of each rope attaches to a truck tire. Six of them lay flat against the trailer's sides. Their weight apparently holds the tarp in place when it storms.

The outhouse is a wooden affair, propped up on one side by two wooden planks. I'd hate to be inside when it tips over.

I'm fascinated. This world is far, far away from my comfy office in downtown Boston. It's more like being in a sci-fi movie, except the special effects are real.

Russell knocks on the torn screen door. A thin white-bearded elf person appears wearing khaki shorts, scuffed brown boots, grey socks with red trim, and a gold Bulova wristwatch. A series of black straps crisscross his bare chest and shoulders, holding the hook onto his right arm where his hand used to be, before the logging accident many years ago. He looks to be at least one hundred years old, even though he's in his seventies, with skin like tanned deer hide. It's Larry.

"Hey, Old Man. How're ya doin'?" Russ says. "I brought my little sister to meet you."

"Come on in. Little sister, you come on in too. You can sit over there but let me move a couple things out of your way first." His voice is surprisingly gentle.

Larry slowly ambles toward a built-in ripped cushion bench at the back of the RV that's covered in pots and bowls. I carefully step over more white buckets filled with rocks submerged in a strong-smelling liquid. I try to act normal as I pass through the filthy kitchen in which an electric frying pan sits on the counter with a quarter inch of bacon grease coagulating on the bottom. I can't help but notice that some critter, about the size of a pack rat, had walked through it and left footprints.

Every inch of his place is covered in cans, jars, and pans filled with rock and liquid. A doorless refrigerator is storage for more junk. "Want a cookie?" Larry asks, waving an open package of Oreos at me.

"Gee, thanks, but we just ate lunch, and I'm full. What's in all these buckets?"

"Gold." He grins when my eyes turn to saucers. "Those rocks are sittin' in a mixture of water and cyanide to leach out the gold from the ore. I use mercury too, but I keep those buckets outside."

Larry offers a magnifying glass. I look a little closer and spot some brilliant sparkles in the toxic liquid, while trying to not bump the containers and trying hard not to breathe in the fumes.

He tells us about the nerve damage in his remaining hand. Russ told me earlier that Larry will reach into a pan of quicksilver and let the liquid metal balls roll around in his palm. I silently wonder if the mercury he plays with has contributed to his nerve problem. Then he talks about his gold mine and how he's worried about claim jumpers. "My claim is filed with the BLM, but that land is open to the public, and anyone can go up there." Russell asks Larry's permission to take me up there tomorrow. "Sure. But watch out for that last leg of the mountain road."

Our visit concludes quickly after Larry says, "Rattlesnake, a big 'un, got in here a couple days ago, slithered right under that bench you're sittin' on. Haven't seen him since. I'm not goin' after him. I'll just leave him alone. Those things can go for a long time with nothin'."

My legs curl up under me. I shoot a frantic look at Russell. "I think my sister's freaked out by the snake. We gotta go, Larry."

He walks us outside. We pass a wooden boxcar with no roof and no wheels. Larry walks in, and we watch as he releases a rope and lowers something to the level of his chest. It's a ham shank, and it's covered in green mold. Larry slices off a piece with a machete he pulls out of his boot. "Want some? It's real good. I keep it hangin' up high so the mountain lions don't get it."

Well now, I'm about to die on the spot. Larry pops the green morsel into his mouth. "Penicillin. Good for what ails you."

On the way back to Mel's, Russell says, "He's the toughest old bird I've ever met."

At night, alone, I think about Larry. The tough old bird. How is it that he has survived, and my son has not?

April 6, 2004   Snake River, Eastern Oregon

IT'S MEL'S DAY TO distract me. He takes me up to Larry's gold mine on his green Bombardier ATV. The climb begins on a dirt road along a raging stream, which we cross twice. We pass small abandoned mines, some covered by sheets of metal, some gaping holes in the mountainside. More abandoned mines, larger ones, are along the way, each leaving a wretched mess of rusting bulldozers, dredgers, and miscellaneous machinery scattered across the landscape.

We leave the road and junk behind and drive higher across grassy rolling hills, past clumps of leftover winter snow and emerging spring flowers. My head swivels back and forth taking in the natural beauty that stretches seemingly forever over this mountain wilderness. Mother Nature works its magic. I'm in my element here, feeling calm.

"Keep your eyes peeled for bear and mountain lions," Mel says. "They can get ornery if we surprise them."

Yikes. I tighten my grip on the ATV.

We maneuver through multiple switchbacks, nothing too scary until we reach Larry's base camp at six thousand feet, which resembles his domicile—filled with old rotting chairs, white buckets, huge pieces of machinery, rusting cars, and garbage. Lots of garbage.

"Okay, the next part is hairy. Hang on," Mel says.

This next stretch is what Larry was talking about when he said, "Watch out for that last leg of the mountain." In front of us are sixty feet of deep and very loose uphill gravel. The stones are larger than road gravel, the edges are sharp, and they are not packed down, so they don't hold together very well. I can't even call it a road, but a "way" to the top of this mountain. The grade is so steep, I'm afraid we'll topple over backwards.

I take one look and yell, "Stop! Let me off! There's no way I'm driving up that road of death!" Mel stops, and I carefully get off the ATV. I take a few deep breaths, trying to stave off a panic attack.

I'm already thinking about the way down, because at the bottom of this treacherous "way," where I am now standing, is a sharp hairpin turn with a tiny landing. If you're going too fast or don't angle your vehicle just right, you will go off the cliff, become airborne, and take a fast trip six thousand feet straight down to the bottom of the mountain.

"I'll walk up. See you at the top." My feet sink into the rocks. I slip several times but make it to the summit. Mel guns the ATV and, with rocks flying, barely makes it up. "I think I'll have to spend the rest of my life up here," I say, "because there's no way I'm going down. If I slip, like I did on the way up, it'll be all over."

"Take a look at this view," he says.

His distraction works. I gaze out over the tranquil Snake River, the desolate mountains on the other side in Idaho, the vast unspoiled vista, and my panic evaporates.

Then I turn around and look at the junk pit that is Larry's mine. First thing I see is a huge yellow excavator, like they use for highway construction. "How on earth did he get that monster up here?"

"Very carefully," says Mel.

There is more junk strewn around—slightly less than below, but still disgusting. Mel walks me over to a pit thirty feet long by twenty feet wide, dug into pure rock, and at least thirty feet deep. "This is it—Larry's White Bucket Mine. He's been working this for seventeen years."

"Holy cow! I've never seen anything like this. What has he found? Lots of gold?"

"He'll never say. One rule about gold mining—you keep to yourself. There are plenty of people who would love to take you out and take it over for themselves. Just like that. They hear about a big strike, and you're toast."

We take one last look around before I skooch my way down the death road on my butt. I can't watch as Mel inches down in a controlled skid, his knuckles white on the brakes. Once he's around the hairpin and safely away from the edge, I get on the ATV and don't look back.

Halfway down the mountain, he stops. "Okay, little sister, you take over getting us home. I'll teach you how to work this thing."

He shows me the basics. I start cautiously until I get the hang of it, then let it rip when we hit the dirt road along the river. "Woo hoo! This is awesome!" I shout as we speed recklessly along.

Something deep and buried is releasing within me. The horror of the past ten months is shaking loose. It feels so good to step beyond the debilitating grief, to really let go and be wild and crazy for a little while.

My brother is standing on the porch when I zip into the driveway and screech to a halt. "Oh my god, it's you driving like that! All I saw was a cloud of dust and heard yelling over the roar of the motor. I was going to kill Mel for being so out of control with you on that thing! What the hell!"

"Don't worry. It was me. I had to let go. Release all that stress and sadness. Those few wild minutes were total freedom and joy. I needed that."

The next morning, Russ comes into the kitchen from outside. His face is pale. "You won't believe this. I was halfway down the driveway on Mel's ATV just now, and the brakes went out! Holy shit! You two were up the mountain on that thing. Oh, my god."

I think about Mel maneuvering down from the gold mine, the dangerous hairpin landing, and me gunning it crazily on the narrow river road. If the brakes had gone out then ...

Two years later, as Larry was coming down the death road in his Chevy, his luck gave out. Did the brakes or engine fail? Was it a claim jumper who sabotaged his truck? Did he miscalculate the hairpin turn? No one knows the details, but Larry went sailing off into the blue in his Chevy truck and took the short and final way down.

Another light gone out in the world.

**

As I fly away from Oregon, my mind and heart are filled with gratitude and love for my brother, his family, and his friends who introduced me to a world so different and so fascinating that my mind was more occupied with taking it all in, than with grieving.

PART IV

MASSACHUSETTS

CHAPTER 51

Mother's Day

May 9, 2004   Annisquam, Massachusetts

HE WOULD HAVE CALLED by now, and a pink azalea plant in pink foil with a matching bow would have been delivered with a card that read, "Happy Mother's Day, Mom. I love you, Rob."

Deep in my mind, tucked into a corner under heavy cover, I'm clinging to an irrational hope that the flowering plant from Rob might arrive, even though I know this is downright crazy. But then I have become a little crazy, fighting with my psyche, trying to help it understand that Rob is gone. Gone. And not coming back. But my mind is fighting against this information, and it's disrupting me into secretly hoping for that azalea. Everything is so convoluted in my head. I'm not even sure this paragraph makes any sense. But that's the point—nothing makes sense.

Maybe Angel will call. Maybe she will send a plant, knowing that's what Rob used to do. Does a mother-in-law count on Mother's Day? I'm hoping I do, but I don't know, because I'm new to this. And so is she.

Shannon drove up to Annisquam last night with her kitty. He loves the open space and hardwood floors in my living room where he can run like he's possessed, then slide sideways as he rounds the corner toward the bedrooms. He makes us laugh.

This morning, she and I sipped mimosas as we made waffles from scratch and topped them with fresh raspberries drenched in Vermont maple syrup. For dinner she's making coq au vin. The Veuve Clicquot is chilling in the 'fridge. I'm so happy we have each other to celebrate Mother's Day. We cling to each other knowing what we have lost, knowing how important we are to each other, especially now. Rob taught us that.

And that lesson will be my Mother's Day gift from him.

CHAPTER 52

Guilt

May 25, 2004   Annisquam, Massachusetts

As PARENTS, WE MAKE mistakes raising our children. My mom spanked me when I veered off the path of accepted behavior. I thought this was normal. (I did have one occasion when I thought I must have been adopted because no birth mother would be so cruel.) Spanking was considered acceptable, or so I believed. So, when occasionally Rob veered off the path of accepted behavior, I swatted him, and he cried.

Now that I have witnessed all the pain and suffering he endured over his last ten months of life, the guilt I feel for every spank, for every misstep in parenting, for every time he cried because of me, eats away at me. How I wish I could rewind the clock and change my views on discipline, replace my mistakes with enlightened behaviors, take every tear away from my sweet little boy.

Before he died, I asked Rob to forgive me for my mistakes in raising him. "Mom, there's no need for any forgiveness. You did the best you knew how," was his blessing to me. I am grateful he was so understanding, but it didn't take my guilt away.

I realize I need more help with managing grief than my friends and family can give. I ask around and find Alice P comes highly recommended as a therapist. The recommendations are accurate. Her demeanor is calm, with a spark in her eye that tells me she enjoys life. She gestures me into her office, decorated much like my living room—bright with natural light, a cushy couch in soft shades of blue with white and peach throw pillows, and lots of plants. Immediately, I feel at home and sense I have come to the right place.

"Tell me why you're here," she says.

My protective shield melts away, the tears come, and I recount the horrors of the past ten months. She takes it all in, her eyes never leaving mine.

After a few weeks of talking with her, I feel safe enough to open up about my guilt for not being the perfect parent. I tell her all the scenarios that have kept me awake at night, tell her how I asked Rob for his forgiveness and he gave it, but it didn't take my remorse away. She listens, looks at me, waits until we are deeply connected eye to eye, then says, "You have to forgive yourself."

This is a breakthrough moment. These simple five words, "You have to forgive yourself," have a profound effect on me. Suddenly everything shifts in my head. It's as if I'm standing in an entirely new location and looking at myself from a new perspective, one I've never noticed, never even considered before. The tight straps of guilt begin to loosen their grip, and I can see freedom ahead.

I can forgive myself. And I will. It may take a little time, but I will.

CHAPTER 53

What's Real?

June 6, 2004   Annisquam, Massachusetts

I'M BETTER, BUT I'M not. Rob has been gone nearly four months now. New levels of reality seep into my brain. Each is deeper, more disheartening, and painful beyond the moon. It's the simple things I miss—no more "Hi Mom!" phone calls on Saturday morning, no more oh so accurate imitations of my dad that made me laugh, no more big Rob smiles that disarmed anyone in his vicinity, no more of anything, because ... I'm trying to say, "because he is dead," but those words are too harsh, too vividly real. "Dead" forces me to look squarely at the truth, but I can't. Not yet.

I sit in my house alone, stare out the window, but see nothing and cry from depths previously unknown. Nothing is important anymore. Everything seems superficial and phony. Conversations, getting showered and dressed, eating, all require energy I no longer have.

The only things I truly value are love and my children. And one of them is gone. My faith, my beliefs, my spirituality now seem like parlor games, tricks of the mind to get me through the troubled spots in life. Before Rob died, I thought I knew all about the soul and how it goes on, but watching Rob in his death experience and praying for divine intervention that never came, I realize expecting a miracle was a fantasy. I'm angry I was taken in, angry I had hope when there was none.

The "Buzz buzz, Mr. Bumble Bee" message is comforting on one level, but confusing and disturbing on another. If I don't believe, how can I accept this? Is he on another plane of existence and reaching out, or am I so in need of connection with him that I'm taken in once again?

And how do I explain what happened yesterday when I went into the depths of my basement, closed the door and screamed, cried, and raged until I thought I would throw up. I wanted to pick up all the glass jars filled with screws on my workbench and smash them against the cement wall. As I reached for one, I felt an arm slide across my shoulders. The touch was real and instantly comforted me. My hysteria vanished. I felt calm and filled with love. Someone was holding me, but no one was there.

Shannon calls to tell me about the dreams she has been having over the past few weeks. "Rob comes to me and takes me flying. No plane, just flying. We float off into the clouds. It's hyper-real, like it's not a dream, like it's actually happening. We've taken off together several times. It was really good."

There is a history in my family of some sort of extra-sensory perception. Shannon has it too, so I don't doubt her.

"Where do you go? Do you talk? What does he say? What's it like?" I ask, eager for any shred of information.

There is a short silence. "If it's okay with you, I'd rather not talk about it. Just know he is helping me," she says, and the conversation is over. My daughter is intensely private. I've tried to get used to it over the years.

I think back to February when Shannon flew to LA for Rob's last birthday. He wasn't happy about having her there. He had never been happy about having her around ever since she was born. That night, in a moment of direct honesty, I asked him if he had any unfinished business.

"No." He looked into my eyes. "Except for Shannon."

"What do you think you're going to do about that?"

"I don't know. What can I do?"

"Tell her you love her."

His eyes froze over. "I won't do that."

I had been gentle and forgiving since he was diagnosed, but this lifelong, unwarranted dislike for his sister prickled me. "I have to say it like it is, Rob. There is no time left for you to continue being unreasonable about this. Think about it. Telling her you love her just might help you let go and get beyond whatever you are holding onto inside. And it would definitely help her. But don't say it unless you mean it."

The next day I saw him take her aside quietly, briefly, but long enough for Shannon to look surprised, a little awkward, then brush her lips across his cheek. The ice between them began to melt.

It seems Shannon's flying dreams are his way to finish his work with her. How can I not believe?

CHAPTER 54

The Gardens

June 8, 2004   Annisquam, Massachusetts

MY GARDENS HAVE BEEN a godsend in the past, a working meditation, but I have no energy, no interest in much of anything, and I have let them go. They are overgrown and filled with weeds, messy, a reflection of my mind.

My sister, Linda, lives in the Chicago suburbs, not far from where we grew up. She wanted to come to LA after Rob died, but I asked her to wait until I was home, because that's when I was really going to need her—when all the activity was settled, and I was alone and trying to face reality.

She holds me close at the airport. A sense of relief seeps in. Someone who has known me and loved me from my first day on earth is here. We gather her luggage and head north to Cape Ann. As we pull into my driveway, I see her eyes widen in alarm as she takes in my front yard. She's a first-rate gardener, never a leaf out of place or a wilted plant at her house. My yard looks like a scene from the children's book, *Where the Wild Things Are*, and I don't care.

"Wow!" She says, "Looks like someone kidnapped your gardener! Have you gotten any ransom notes?"

I appreciate her humor. Criticism would finish me off. What I need is gentleness and love, and she brings that with her. In addition to hugs, she expresses her affection for me in another way, by pulling on some work gloves and stepping into the chaos.

First thing the next morning, I find her outside talking to the greenery, yanking weeds, stepping back to assess, yanking more weeds, snipping, fine tuning, restoring my beautiful gardens to their happiest state.

"Look at this," she says, pointing to the overgrown pink rhododendron bush by my front door. "Buzz buzz, Mr. Bumble Bee." The bush is swarming with fat bees, their legs heavy with yellow pollen.

"I've only seen a few bees from time to time on this bush. Never anything like this. There must be hundreds of them!" I stop and listen to the incredible sound vibrating through the air, a lovely humming symphony. "Do you think ... I want it to be ... Could it be a message from Rob?" Ridiculous. But, maybe.

We let that mystical possibility dangle in the air and exchange a sisterly glance. We each know what's in the other's mind—of course this is from Rob.

Noticing actual earth around the flowers instead of wilderness, I ask, "How long have you been out here?"

"Long enough to get a good start. Why don't you join me?"

I feel a tinge of interest, but my energy is too low. "Maybe later," I say and wander across the yard and down the four rough granite stairs into the vacant lot next to my house. I have purposely left this area wild. White birch, pine, and oak scent the air. Layers of brown curled leaves are deep and crunchy under my feet. Patches of blue bells peek out from under them. Mushrooms grow from tree stumps. My Transcendentalist self feels a connection, and a bit of life comes back into me. I consider freeing some of these wildflowers from their blanket of leaves, but not yet. I'm content to know they are there, buried, but still vibrant under their shroud of oak.

"I'll get us some tea," I say to my sister as I emerge from my retreat, cross the lawn and pass the rhododendron bush. The swarm of bumble bees has moved on. And so must I.

CHAPTER 55

On the Move

June 16, 2004   Waldoboro, Maine

MY PHONE RINGS. IT'S Marilee, my gal pal, who I met twen-
ty-plus years ago when we were both antique dealers.

"If you're not doing anything this weekend, let's go to Farnsworth. I have to open the house for the season, and I'd love to
have your company. Plus, I intend to put you to work."

My friends are clever in providing what they think I won't
realize is a distraction. I load my suitcase into Marilee's Saab,
and we set off on the one hundred-and-eighty-five-mile trip to
her family's summer house, Farnsworth, built in 1760 on what
appears to be a zillion acres of land on the rocky Maine coast.

The usual three-hour drive is more like six because we are
both addicted to TJ Maxx and have to stop at every location
along the way in search of bath towels to match the three she
bought at TJ Maxx in Boston last week. Then there is the pause
at Moody's Diner where we have lunch and load up on their
famous Four Berry Pie. We each devour a wedge while sitting
at the counter, buy two more for late night snacks, and an additional two for breakfast. That should hold us until we stop at
Moody's on the way home.

The house has been closed up since November and is musty inside. Marilee struggles to open the sash-style windows, nine original panes on top, nine on the bottom, but they are stuck. Moisture from spring rains, age, and humidity bloat the wooden frames, so they require some finesse in bumping them with the heel of the hand just right, so they move without breaking the glass. I manage to open a few while she does the rest. Salty air pours in and refreshes the house.

We walk outside to survey the overgrown lawn and gardens, assessing the work that awaits us in the morning, then head over to the barn to make sure we have garden tools and gas for the lawn mower. Check and check.

Memories hit hard at the most unexpected times. The tears come when I spot a stand of trees between the barn and the Atlantic. Wide grayish-brown vertical strips of bark curl at the edges. They're sugar maples, a familiar New England sight.

We had two such trees, over one hundred years old, in our yard in Weston, Massachusetts, where Rob and Shannon spent their early years. Every spring, Bill McElwain, a Harvard-educated farmer and activist living among high-powered executives and sports figures (I almost ran over Bobby Orr one day, but that's another story), rounded up the Middle School kids and tapped all the sugar maples around town. I remember Rob hopping out of the trailer attached to the back of Bill's turquoise Toyota Land Cruiser, proudly hammering a couple spouts into our trees, hanging buckets to catch the drippings, then hopping back into the trailer, the other kids happily slapping him on the back for a job well done.

Twice a week the turquoise Toyota, filled with kids, made the rounds to empty hundreds of pails, each near to overflowing with watery liquid. They hauled the sap to the Sugar Shack, a rustic building behind the school, built by Bill and the kids a few years before. Here the 13-year-olds tossed split wood into a roaring fire under evaporator tanks where they boiled down the trees' bounty into maple syrup. Over six weeks, they reduced ten thousand gallons of sap to a couple hundred gallons of syrup.

In early April Rob invited us to a Sugar-On-Snow party, the grand finale to the sugaring off season. "Wait here. I'll get your plates," he said as we lingered with other parents outside the wooden shack that smelled heavenly. "Here you go," he said proudly as he handed over plates piled with fresh snow imported from Vermont. On top of the snow was a generous drizzling of maple syrup, hardened by the cold snow. A slice of dill pickle sat next to the treat.

"A pickle?" I asked. "What's this pickle doing here?"

"It's to cut the sweetness of the sugar. Try it." He was so excited, he could hardly wait for me to taste the results of his hard work, then bite into the pickle.

"Oh my gosh, this is delicious!"

A sweet smile broke across his eager face.

"Are you all right?" Marilee asks when she notices my tears.

"Just having a fond memory of Rob."

We take a few steps to the water's edge and stroll along the shore, taking in the pristine beauty all around us. We stop to watch at least forty horseshoe crabs in various stages of marital bliss in the shallows by the beach. What strange prehistoric creatures they are, their hard shells clacking as they bump into each other, searching for the perfect mate. Then we head back to the house where I retreat to my room, read, and fall into a peaceful sleep.

A cup of tea and a slice of Four Berry Pie, while still in my jammies and slippers, are the perfect start to the day. We linger at the antique kitchen table, talking, but it's over too soon. "It's time to attack," Marilee says, referring to the overgrown mess outside.

"I'll be ready in a few." I'm looking forward to getting my hands and clothes dirty and breaking a sweat. Not only will it work off some of Moody's calories, but trying to tame Mother Nature is both satisfying and therapeutic.

I've been mowing ankle high grass for two-and-a-half hours and have barely dented the expanse. Marilee is pulling weeds, trying to restore what used to be the garden. A blister is forming on the pad of my right hand, and my arms hurt from pushing the mower forward then pulling it back to untangle the grass from the blade, but I ignore it and carry on, determined to at least clear the area around the house today and not succumb to idleness. I imagine the people who lived here in 1760 and what it was like for them to maintain this place. No power tools, just a strong Puritan work ethic. I double down and keep at it, as does my friend.

The day flies by, and I feel physically exhausted, but happy. I barely stay awake during dinner, then fall into bed, listening to the sound of the ocean for only a few minutes before I drop into a deep sleep.

Sunday, we celebrate our outdoor accomplishments with a trip to Rockland to see the Farnsworth Art Museum and The Wyeth Center, where three generations of that talented family's paintings are on display. We stop at Moody's Diner on the way home and repeat our Friday gustatory adventure, only this time I go for the rhubarb-strawberry pie. We make only one stop at a TJ Maxx we missed on the way up.

I return to Annisquam, content for the moment with the hard work and the pleasant memory that brought me back to Rob as a happy young boy. Perhaps the tide is turning, and some of my grief will lighten up as it did this past weekend in Maine.

CHAPTER 56

Sleepless

June 20, 2004   Annisquam, Massachusetts

I WENT INTO BOSTON to Lee Hecht Harrison today for a seminar, "Getting Back Into the Job Market," but it turns out the fast-paced energy in Boston along with the energy needed to find a job were too much for me. I came home exhausted. I hate the city's filth, the bad air, and the brusque people. I'm concerned I won't be able to work again. I can't concentrate. I don't care about much of anything. I don't even want to be employed anymore, especially in the anxiety-producing arena I was in at the bank. But I have to have a job. What's out there for me? My thoughts run into dead ends and eventually into tangles with no answers. "I have to" vs. "I can't" creates more anxiety.

Tonight, I'm edgy and tired. At eleven I'm in bed and fall gently into a pre-sleep state, that place where I'm not fully asleep, but not fully awake. Sleep is near until a vivid picture of Rob exhaling his last breath creeps in. I'm wide awake.

I get up, wrap myself in a blanket, and wander out to the living room in the dark with just enough light from the moon so I don't bump my toes on the furniture. How can I get my mind off the image of his lifeless body? Mindless late-night TV might do it. Jimmy Kimmel tries to make me laugh but fails. I watch, not listening, until my eyes glaze over and restlessness propels me back to my bed.

My joints hurt. So do my lower back, thumbs, left shoulder, knees, and hips. I'm worried about my body. What's wrong with me? What if I die right this minute—a major heart attack and boom, I'll be gone. Or maybe it will be a slow and painful death from cancer, like Rob. Can it be that he's really dead?

This has got to stop, or I'll be useless tomorrow. I have to shift my thoughts. Since Rob died, I've stopped the grateful journal because most nights I can't come up with anything for which I am grateful. I notice it's raining, so I focus on the steady cadence of raindrops on my roof to quiet my mind. It works. Then I try a relaxation technique and focus on my toes—consciously relaxing them one by one, then move to the soles and tops of my feet, my ankles, my calf muscles, my knees and so on up my body. By the time I get to my waist, my mind has shifted to calm, and I feel sleep quietly taking over.

CHAPTER 57

On the Move Again

July 19, 2004   Nantucket, Massachusetts

OH, LOVELY NANTUCKET. I'M leaving in the morning for a four-day visit to that tiny island in the Atlantic where Kathryn lives. I'm hoping to relax with her in the studio above the garage and listen to her read from the book she is writing, *The Gilder.* I'm looking forward to hearing how ideas drop magically into her head out of nowhere—well, maybe from some related life experiences or observations—then turn into a series of interconnected scenes, which materialize into a vibrant story in a novel, and eventually land on a bookstore shelf. Her readers will find themselves lost in artistic and passionate escapades in Florence, Italy.

Inklings of coming change, stepping beyond grief (is that possible?), and moving back into my life are sneaking into my thoughts. I know I will get some help on these topics while I'm here. Kathryn is a dear friend who is savvy about women's issues, relationships, and taking care of one's self. She is loyal and caring, always full of support and wisdom. She has never failed to help untangle my thoughts and provide new ones for me to consider.

I'm hoping to get some cheerleading from her about identifying and using my own strengths. Not working has been lovely, but empty, and grieving has been, well, painful and debilitating. Perhaps I am expecting too much from this little trip, when what I really need and want most is friendship—to connect on a soul level with my friend who knows me well and will guide me with kindness.

The drive to the ferry is a thoughtful one. Each town I pass evokes memories from some part of my 35 years in Massachusetts. As I cross over the Bourne Bridge, the landscape changes, and I know I'm on Cape Cod. Boston's full-sized trees shrink into Lilliputians here because of the sandy soil. There is a different quality to the light, it's brighter, and the sky is bluer. The air is sweet and clean. Gentleness abounds on The Cape, except on Friday afternoons during the summer, when the roads are choked with cars idling in standstill traffic, dumping clouds of exhaust into the air. Weekend tranquility shatters into nerve-wracking desperation to get to the beach house or to the Hy-Line ferry before it leaves. But today is Monday, so I ease on down the road.

My thoughts drift to larger questions about life. Since Rob's passing, I've lost focus, lost my sense of purpose as a mortal on this planet. Why am I here? Was I born for a reason—to do something or be something? What about Rob? Why was he here for such a short time? Did he fulfill his purpose then leave, satisfied? He fought death until he couldn't fight anymore. What is death anyway? Where did he go? His life force was here one second, then gone the next. What will my death be like and when will it come? Will he be there, waiting for me on the other side? What is the other side, if there is one? I just don't know.

I simply want to be happy again.

As I near the waterfront in Hyannis I need to concentrate on where I'm going. Small green signs with images of ships direct me to either the Hy-Line, which has the smaller but faster ferry to Nantucket, or the Steamship Authority, a behemoth that's slow and solid in the water. Today the Hy-Line will get my business. The water is calm, so the sail will be smooth, an important factor for those of us who suffer from mal de mer.

A few years ago, I made the terrible error of taking the fast ferry during a storm. Once beyond the calm waters of the harbor and out to the churning sea, I think I was the first passenger to turn a sickly green. Plastered into my chair on the outer deck, not moving a muscle except to gasp bits of fresh air, I felt nausea rising fast. "Wastebasket," I barked while jabbing my finger toward the nearest container. "Get it! Quick!" My chalky sweating face told the unfortunate person who was sitting next to me to not delay. Oblivious to its slightly grimy exterior and mixed contents, I clutched the container to my chest like an old friend and filled it until I was empty.

My stay on Nantucket is everything I need, from the pale peach roses Kathryn picked from her secret garden and placed next to my bed, to walks along the sandy beach where she asked poignant questions that set me to thinking beyond my misery, to riding bikes into town where we sat at the counter at Two Steps Up and ate eggs Benedict while talking nonstop.

I board the homebound ferry on Thursday morning, my carry-on bag filled with fresh loaves of Portuguese Sweet Bread from Something Natural, a Nantucket Nectars lemonade, and a lighter heart.

Alone

August 17, 2004   Annisquam, Massachusetts

LIFE'S ACTIVITIES ARE OVER for the day. As I switch the lighted room to darkness and sink dreamily into my pillows to chase sleep, it hits me. My eyelids, once heavy and finished for the day, snap open. Reality assaults me hard and painfully deep—irrational and scary thoughts hidden in my sub-conscious spill out.

I am alone. Alone in my oversized bed, alone in my house, alone in this city, in this life. And the what ifs begin. They start easy and typical, then build.

What if something happens to me? Who would know? What if that branch that crackled outside is not the woodchuck or the coyote, but some kook or druggie with ill will on his mind? What if he slits my screen and gets into my room before the alarm brings help? What if my alarm company is just another corporation that overworks and overstresses its employees into inefficient service or no service at all? What if I have a heart attack and can't get to my phone? Do I even know the symptoms of a heart attack? They're different in women. What if I'm having a heart attack, and I think it's just that I ate too much at dinner tonight, and I ignore it? What if my heart stops beating, like Rob's?

Rob. I can't get the picture of his lifeless body out of my mind. I can't get the pain out of my heart. He was only 35. I'm 55, his mom. Why not me instead? I've lived long enough, and he was just getting started. My son, my child. Damn, damn evil cancer. I caught mine early. I barely thought about it because my focus was on my dying child. Now the thoughts are creeping in. What if that pain in my lower back is more cancer?

Where is he? I thought I knew a lot about the afterlife, about a lot of things. I know nothing. What used to be important no longer has meaning. It's fluff. Ego fabrication.

Hundreds of crickets serenade the night. I know as long as they sing their song that no one or no thing is nearby. They go silent when apparent danger is near. Acorn bombs from the giant oak hit my deck and roof, each one jarring me a little at first, and then I stop hearing them. The owl's eerie trill makes the hairs on my arms stand up. Mom always scared the bejesus out of me, warning in that low ominous voice intended to impress, "The owl's call means death."

I gave Rob a stuffed owl with furry wings and an orange beak on his first birthday. In his last weeks of life, I told his wife and friends the story about him sharing his first birthday cake with Owl by pressing a frosted piece of cake into its felt beak. He paused, then he squashed the cake onto his own forehead. We all laughed, then Angel disappeared from the room. When she returned, she was holding a rag tag clump with a mangled orange protrusion and one furry wing. "Is this Owl?" Rob was that kind of amazing guy who, in a box he labeled "Ephemera," saved all his grandmother's letters, his winning Boy Scout Pinewood Derby racer, and his owl.

I can't stop my thoughts. If I could snuggle up to someone I love, be held tightly in their arms, cry, and unburden my badly damaged heart that would help. But I am alone.

I can't think. I can't make decisions. Losing Rob has left a deep, deep emptiness in me that nothing can ever fill. Time. I need time to heal.

It's finally sunrise. I dress and walk to the ocean through the misty fog. It hangs heavy like my eyelids and my heart. I walk away from trying to find sleep and step into this new day, fresh like each wave that washes the grains of sand, and begin to fill it with distracting activities.

CHAPTER 59

Support

September 28, 2004 Annisquam, Massachusetts

I FEAR FOR MY sanity. Even though I have intervals of distraction and days that seem somewhat normal, it's not enough. I somehow make it through each day, but when I go to bed, just after my head hits my pillow, and I take a deep breath to relax into sleep, all the pain, the agony, the intense feelings of loss come rushing out of that dark place where they live, and I'm awake. I lie there for I don't know how long. "Get up when you can't sleep," all the literature says, but I feel too heavy to move and have no energy to motivate myself. As the moon moves steadily through the night sky, I watch the shadows from the dogwood tree outside my window move slowly across my blanket.

Nature's urge forces me to get up. Any unnatural light will awaken me further, so I leave the bathroom overhead off.

Still in the dark, I walk into the living room and stare blankly into the treetops, then move into the kitchen where I stop to contemplate the moon through the skylight. It's nearly full tonight. Moonlight casts an eerie glow across the cabinets and onto the refrigerator, specifically onto the eight-by-ten black-and-white photo of a smiling Rob, held in place with heart-shaped magnets. I stare at his handsome face, his broad, engaging smile, and the spirited energy in his very alive eyes. But I have no smiles in me to return. My chest heaves as emotion rises. It turns my stomach, attacks my heart, burns my throat, and chokes me until I set it free with an inhuman wail.

I need help.

Last November, I went to a support group at Mass Gen Hospital in Boston. It was too much at the time. I wasn't ready. Alice, my therapist, is wonderful, but now I need to talk with other parents who have lost their adult children. I want to know if they are going as crazy as I am, how they survive each day, and I need to hear the stories of what happened to their son or daughter.

Hospice is helpful when I call. They direct me to a support group specifically for parents who have lost adult children. "It's best to wait at least six months before joining a support group," they tell me. "A new group, one that will meet your needs, is starting on Cape Ann next week." The timing is good—it's been almost seven months since Rob died. I sign on.

As I walk into the austere church basement activity room, I am slightly agog to see seven other people already seated around the table. For some unknown reason, I truly thought I was the only one in this situation, that no other family had suffered such an unnatural loss. But here are seven others who live within twenty miles of me.

The overhead fluorescent lighting casts harsh shadows on their tired faces. But maybe it's not only the light, maybe they're just as haggard as I am. As I get closer to the group, I'm surprised to see a woman I knew socially a couple years back. "What are you doing here?" I ask.

"My son died," she said, her voice wobbly.

"Oh, no. I'm so sorry. I lost my son also."

"I heard that from Joe. It must have been awful." She stands up, and we hug.

"Welcome. I'm Andrea," says a middle-aged woman at the head of the table. "I'll be leading the group." I give her my name and settle into the last available folding chair. She checks me off a list.

Andrea looks directly at each of us as her eyes move around the table. "I'm so glad you're here tonight. Reaching out for support when you're in the depths of grief is not always easy. But you've done it. And, by reaching out, you are no longer alone with your grief. You're now with a group of kindred spirits. Each of you has lost a child, an adult, but still your child." She pauses to let that sink in. "We are here for the next six weeks to help and support each other through the grieving process."

Andrea leans forward in her chair. "When you signed up for this group, we asked you to make a commitment to attend all six sessions. Now that we are together, I would like each of you to speak that commitment out loud to the group. This is an important step in our bonding together, our commitment to making this a safe space, and our commitment to respecting and supporting each other."

After we voice promises around the table, Andrea invites us to introduce ourselves, tell our son or daughter's name, tell when and how they died, and show their photo we were asked to bring. We pass the pictures around one at a time. When it's my turn, I tell them, "This is my son, Rob Mulloy. He was 35 when he died seven months ago from stomach cancer." Each person holds Rob's image and studies him carefully. Silently they pass him to the next parent, then look at me with eyes that say, "I feel your loss."

With each photo and each brief story, a camaraderie takes hold in the group—we now have a better understanding that our words and emotions relate to real people, to our children. We have each seen what the others have lost.

Everyone else's son or daughter died suddenly. Double car accident—T-boned by one car, then immediately T-boned by a second car at age 24. Suicide—hanged himself in the garage at age 31. Heart attack—died while napping on the couch at age 22. Car accident—head on collision at age 40. Head trauma—fell off a ladder while cleaning the gutters and hit his head on a landscape rock at age 62.

I'm the only one whose son knew he was going to die, had time to settle his affairs, and time to say goodbye, an opportunity the others wish their son or daughter had. But I'm also the only one who watched my child struggle through incredible emotional and physical agony as he slowly died over a period of ten months, something for which most are grateful they didn't have to witness. We don't even venture toward a discussion about which might be worse because they're all horrific. From a parents' perspective, there is no good way for our children to die. They shouldn't have died at all.

We each tell more about our children, about who we are, and how our lives have been impacted by their death. Some open up easily and are grateful for the opportunity to release their feelings in a safe place. Some are more reserved and hold their feelings back. But everyone reaches for a Kleenex at some point because this is not easy stuff.

I feel especially tender toward an older gentleman who can't understand why his son, age 62, pre-deceased him. "What do I have to live for?" he says. "I'm 84 and all done with living. Sam was just getting ready to retire and have some fun." He hits a nerve with several in the group. We talk about the myth of believing death comes only in old age and certainly not before a parent. I tell how I prayed, "Please take me, and let him live." And how I thought maybe my cancer might be my prayer being answered, but it wasn't.

Andrea introduces Kubler-Ross' Five Stages of Grief—Denial. Anger. Bargaining. Depression. Acceptance. She briefly describes each one, noting the belief that a parent should not bury their child can be found in each of the first four stages, manifesting in various ways. "Sitting here with eight people who have outlived their children makes a strong statement that this is a myth. But beliefs die hard, and we're here to help each other move through them and heal.

"It's normal for us to be all over the place in terms of Kubler-Ross' stages," she continues. "The lines between them can be blurry. And not everyone experiences all five stages or even experiences them in the same order. Some go back and forth among the stages. Think about where you might be now and where you have been. We'll talk more about that next time." And she draws the group to a close.

Driving home along the dark streets, I am grateful for this gathering of parents who suffer as I do and who, by joining this group, may be ready to start the healing process too. And begin to heal in the company of others who understand. And not try to do it alone.

CHAPTER 60

One More Update

August 3, 2004   Los Angeles, California

ANGEL SEEMS TO BE doing much better than I am. She and Rob received an ample cash wedding gift from Aunt Cindi and Uncle Gary for a mind-blowing honeymoon. Angel planned it and went alone. She sent this update after she returned to LA.

—

... Rob's illness took a toll on all of us who loved him. While caring for him over the last year, I kind of forgot myself and no longer knew what I liked or wanted out of life. I'm delighted to tell you this trip has helped me recover and reconnect with myself even more than I thought possible.

I met wonderful new people, experienced amazing places, tastes, and adventures, and had time to heal as well. I met people who helped me open up and work through emotional issues.

In each new place I sprinkled only a small part of Rob's ashes so he could be part of those locations too, and because I wasn't ready to let go. By the time I got to Brazil, I'd had time to reflect, was beginning to feel peace, and was finally ready to release all the contents of the baby powder shaker I was carrying him in. At the top of a mountain, I eased myself onto the tip of the rock outcrop, released Rob's ashes into the wind, and said, "I release you. I free you." It was hard, but in freeing him, I have also freed myself, and a new life is already unfolding.

Love to all of you!

Angel

PART V

CALIFORNIA, MASSACHUSETTS, OREGON

CHAPTER 61

Nightmare Relief

October 5–9, 2004 San Diego, California

I'M BACK IN SAN Diego for a brief visit. Ginger knows I am not sleeping and am traumatized by memories that haunt me at night. She is concerned and taps into her network of flight attendant friends who can answer any question or find a solution to any problem anywhere in the world. She puts my issue out there and gets an answer the next day. "Her name is Nancy. She's a psychotherapist who works with people whose lives have been impacted by trauma," Ginger says. "And she's right here in San Diego, on Banker's Hill near Balboa Park. Here's her number."

"I've been expecting your call," Nancy says. "Are you a flight attendant too?"

"No, just a good friend of one."

"I've been given only a brief sketch of your sleeping problems. Would you like to come in, talk, and see what we can do to help you? Are you familiar with EMDR? That's the modality I use with my trauma patients."

"You come highly recommended, so yes, I would. But I'm not familiar with EMDR."

"It's simple, but powerful. In a nutshell, while you focus on the emotional disturbance, also called the traumatic memory network, I use an external stimulus, usually eye or hand movements to forge a new association between the traumatic memory and more adaptive memories or information."

I'm not really following her, but I figure I'll understand better when I'm experiencing it.

Nancy continues. "What's amazing about this technique is it works. It desensitizes internal and external triggers in 85-90% of single trauma victims. For combat veterans with PTSD, it works in 77% of the cases. I understand you will be in San Diego for a short time. If you're interested, I can clear some space for you, and we can get right to work."

We set up five one-hour sessions. The first is later this afternoon.

In her office, we talk at length about what happened with Rob. I tell her there are two images I have stuck in my mind that haunt me as soon as I get into bed and try to sleep. "The first is the horror of Rob's Cheyne-Stokes breathing. The sound was unbearable, but even worse was when he would stop breathing for several minutes at a time, and I thought he had died. Then, all of a sudden, he would gasp for air, desperate to breathe, frantic to survive. This went on for hours until I was near crazy. It was that desperate gasp for air, his strong life force that wanted to fight back against advancing death that haunts me. Finally, there were no more desperate gasps for breath, and the silence was deafening.

"The other nightmare is an image of Rob my mind conjured. I didn't see this, I only imagined it while I was at the mortuary.

It's his dead body zipped into a plastic bag on the top shelf in a cold storage room, waiting to be cremated.

"These are the images that pop into my head as I'm about to fall asleep. They shock me into full waking and stay with me all night long."

Nancy asks me to take one image at a time. I start with Rob's struggle to breathe, then his not breathing anymore. She tells me to face the image and the feelings head on—to see it and feel it fully and to notice the sensations it causes in my body.

Then she does something strange. She asks me to use only my eyes to follow her hand as she moves it back and forth horizontally and to tell her to stop when the trauma reaches the strongest point. We try it. I'm surprised to notice my feelings deepen and lighten as she moves her hand back and forth. I find the ultimate point and say, "Stop."

"Now I'm going to move my hand vertically, and I want you to do the same thing—use only your eyes, don't move your head, and tell me to stop when the trauma is the strongest. Stay focused on the scene and all the emotions and physical sensations. Don't let your mind wander. Let's begin."

Her hand moves, from the point on the horizontal axis, straight up and down. "Stop," I say when I feel most overwhelmed.

"We've located the place in your brain where the trauma lies. Now we will reprogram that memory with a positive one."

I don't really understand what happened, how she knew where those memories were located in my brain, nor do I understand the whole process. I only know it worked, and I feel some relief. We repeat the process with both images over the next four days, and by the end of the week the trauma has lessened to the point that I can remember these events without feeling overwhelmed. In fact, I can look at them almost objectively. And I'm falling asleep easily when my head hits the pillow at night.

CHAPTER 62

Angel

October 12, 2004   Los Angeles, California

ANGEL MEETS ME FOR lunch near her office. We catch up as we eat, but I notice there is something simmering below her surface that is making her uncomfortable. We leave the restaurant and walk across Rodeo Drive. The highly polished grille of a Rolls Royce flashes in the California sunlight. Winged Victory is ready to take flight, but she has to wait, like the other lesser automobiles, before she can quietly motor on to her destination.

Angel is reserved. This is not like her at all. I know she's formulating something in her head that she wants to say. I break the silence. "I love what you're wearing. It's so ... you."

"Huh? Oh, thanks."

I'm amazed, as usual, at her clothing choices. She mixes colors, textures, and styles in a way unfathomable to me, but it works. It's an ultra-cool Angel flair that screams, "I live in LA, and I'm creative." Today she is wearing a fifties-style rockabilly skirt in stripes of pumpkin and sage with layers of orange crinolines underneath that make the skirt flounce in a wide circle around her with every step. Her blouse is red Chinese silk with frog clasps, and it's topped with a denim jacket and a patterned scarf. Shoes. Who would possibly notice the shoes with all that activity on top?

Rob, on the other hand, was jeans and tees all the way, all the time. Angel did her best to help him with his "look" by sending him to her hairdresser, who produced the latest LA guy-dos. Long sideburns one month, spiky short cut the next. Style in LA is constantly on the move. One should never be caught behind the times.

In the middle of the crosswalk she spills what she has been holding inside. "I have something to say. I hope it won't upset you." Pause. She stops and faces me. "I met someone. And I'm in love."

I stop dead, but the Rolls is now purring as the driver eases it forward with the green light. We hurry to the sidewalk. I'm grateful for the distraction so I can collect myself and think of what to say that sounds cool and calm and won't reveal my complete surprise. I don't want her to pull away from me. "Tell me more," I say.

She looks into my eyes to see if I mean it. "You know I went on the honeymoon Rob and I were supposed to take, only I took my sister on part of it to Edinburgh, Scotland. That's where I met him." She goes on nervously to describe their meeting at a pub, how he and his friend approached and asked if they could join in, and how she found herself laughing, really laughing and talking until the wee Scottish hours.

Her story shakes me up, not because I am unhappy, but because I realize that she is reincarnating. No, not reincarnating, she is more of a phoenix, rising out of her own ashes and into a vibrant new life. She is young, smart, and energetic and able to forge a new scenario for herself.

I, on the other hand, will never have another son, but she will have another husband. She is no longer, "Angel who lost her husband." Her new persona is, "Angel who lost her husband but is moving forward into a new life."

And, where am I? Still at the crossroads, waiting at the light? Or am I, too, beginning to venture out a bit?

CHAPTER 63

A Random Act of Kindness

October 20, 2004   Gloucester, Massachusetts

I FAILED TO NOTICE there was a slow water leak in my exterior door frame, and now the oak threshold between my guest room and its screened-in porch is ruined. I consult Ira, my painter, and the only man around who knows anything about repairs. "You might have trouble finding the exact thing. This threshold was hand milled thirty years ago." He sends me to the Gloucester Building Center on Harbor Loop.

I walk into the store trying not to catch the rotting eight-foot length of wood in the automatic door. A salesman watches my maneuvers. "Hi! Looks like you barely got in without getting whacked by the door. Very skillful. What do you have there?"

Living in a small town pleases me. Most everyone is friendly and helpful, and relationships develop with repeat business. When I lived in Manchester-By-the-Sea, a lifetime ago, my husband, our dog Desert (who names a beach dog Desert?), and I would walk to the hardware store next to the Beach Street Café where we'd launch into a ten-minute gossip fest with Jim the proprietor before getting down to business. Dogs were welcome. In fact, Jim took photos of all the pooches that came in with their owners. Desert's happy face was on the wall at the entrance with twelve others. She would run ahead and wait patiently at the register for one of the Milk Bone treats Jim kept under the counter.

"My painter, Ira, sent me. He thought you guys could help. I'd like to replace this. Can you cut something to match?"

"Oh, Ira. How is he? He was in here a few days ago buying paint. Must have been for your house, huh? Nice colors. Hmm, this oak was hand milled. I'm afraid we don't do custom work like this." He offers several alternatives that don't meet my needs.

As I turn to go, a chubby workman in dusty overalls asks me where I live.

"Annisquam."

"Do you know Rockport?"

"Yes."

"I'm a carpenter. I'm doing a job over there. If you buy the wood and follow me to the house, I'll cut it for you."

Pause. "Really?"

"Yes."

"Okay. Thank you!"

Next thing I know I'm following this guy to Rockport, wondering if I'm crazy, and if this might be a set up for something unsavory, possibly something dangerous. I fret with that thought for a few minutes, then drive behind him down a little-used sandy lane behind a fish store. My anxiety increases. I park and, holding my breath, follow him into a house and up the stairs to the second floor.

As soon as I see the construction activity, I relax. A painter in speckled white pants and cap is priming the walls. He smiles a friendly but curious greeting. I smile in return.

Without speaking a word, the carpenter takes the new eight-foot oak board from me and lays it across some sort of woodworking machine in the middle of the room. Wooden curlicues and sawdust cover the floor beneath it.

"I don't know your name," I say.

"You'll never see me again," he answers slightly annoyed.

Eventually, I get "Steve" out of him.

For the next twenty minutes, I watch in silence as he mills, customizes and sands my board. He finally speaks. "I'm doing this job for a friend," he says. "It should have taken two months, but the plasterers and electricians were slow, and now I'm into my fifth month here. I built the entire second floor of this house to the tune of eighty grand. It would have been a hundred-and-eighty grand if he had hired anyone else.

"I'm a Union carpenter from Saugus. I hate the hour-long commute to Cape Ann. It puts too many miles on my truck. I like to trade it in every three years with low mileage, and this whole project is ruining that."

He turns the machine off and hands me a beautiful replica of my threshold. "Here you go."

"This is so great. Thank you. How much do I owe you?"

"Merry Christmas," he says.

"Really? But ..."

He waves me away.

This random act of kindness from the heart of a stranger touches me deeply. I cry most of the way back to Gloucester.

I pull into Shaw's Grocery, where I pick up ingredients for chocolate chip cookies. I want to do something to say thank you and, with his very round shape, I figure this will be the best way. An hour later, with cookies warm and wrapped in foil, I return to the house in Rockport, go up to the second story, and find Steve working on the floor of a closet with his back to me, his plumber's crack in full view. He jumps when I speak. "You thought you'd never see me again."

I place the package on the floor with a note. I smile at him and leave.

—

Dear Steve,

You have no idea how much your act of kindness means to me. I lost my son to cancer earlier this year and had cancer myself last year (I'm fine now). As a result, I've been feeling pretty low. What you did for me today gave me quite a lift.

I hope these cookies can express some of the thanks (at least a little bit) I feel for the gift you gave me this morning.

With heartfelt thanks,

Ellyn

CHAPTER 64

Another Kindness

October 27, 2004   Gloucester, Massachusetts

FOR THE PAST TWENTY-SOME years, I've had a massage on my birthday. Today is no different.

I'm curled into a cushy leather chair nestled in between two wispy areca palms in the spa waiting area, lounging in a super-soft terry robe and matching slippers, sipping herbal tea. The lights are low and water cascades down a slate fountain, which cancels outside noise. Soothing music floats easily through the room. I am alone with my thoughts until another white terry robe enters through the billowing curtains. She sits opposite me, and we smile at each other.

"Aren't we clever for bringing ourselves here today? Such a treat. Is this your first time having a massage?" she asks.

We slip into a casual conversation, but I'm not much for small talk these days. She asks if I have children, and that does it, tears well in my eyes. One drips onto my cheek. I try to brush it away before she sees it, but I'm too late.

"Is everything all right?"

I shake my head no and open up about Rob's death. I'm losing it, so I try to move toward something positive—the lessons I learned from his death about what's important in life, "Children, Family, Friends, Love. Everything else is pretty much insignificant, not important."

"Ellyn?" A young woman in a white uniform steps in, smiling. "I'm Jean, your masseuse. Are you ready?"

I follow Jean out of the waiting room, escaping the discomfort of crying in front of a perfect stranger. She opens a door and ushers me into a room that smells heavenly, like a lush coco-nutty tropical island. I can almost taste a piña colada. The massage table is covered in soft flannel and radiates warmth from the heated pad below. Relaxation begins immediately and sinks in deeper over the next hour and a half. My masseuse somehow finds exactly where I hold my tension and works deliberately to release the knots in my shoulders, back and neck, then moves professionally over my body, rendering me to near mush. Will I be able to walk?

Jean is waiting outside the room with a glass of water with a lemon slice floating on top. I sip slowly as I make my way to the front desk to settle the bill, my toes feeling slightly slippery inside my shoes. The woman at the register looks at me, checks the appointment schedule, then picks up an envelope. "Are you Ellyn?"

"Yes."

"This is for you. You should read it now."

—

Dear Ellyn (they told me your name at the front counter),

I am paying for your massage today because I think you need something nice to happen to you, an act of kindness by a stranger. Only time can make your pain bearable, but time will make it bearable (not necessarily okay, but bearable). Thank you for your words of wisdom about what matters in life.

Vivienne

Could it be that life is lightening up just a little?

CHAPTER 65

Disaster

November 8, 2004   Annisquam, Massachusetts

THE ROAR OF COLOR that dressed my autumn trees is now vibrant litter blanketing my front yard. Yesterday, the leaves on the maples and the dogwood stood out in shocking color against the sapphire sky. Today they are naked, their dark branches exposed, shivering in the cold morning air. The storm last night must have been a big one, but I slept right through it, oblivious and snug in my cozy bed.

Teacup in hand and comfy in my winter robe, I step onto the back deck and watch the violent black clouds bluster their way out to sea, churning the waves, but leaving a clear blue sky over Annisquam. The pungent smell of soaked fallen leaves and rich wet earth arouse my senses. This is a perfect day for a brisk walk on the beach, I think as I step back inside to refill my cup.

Fond memories of past storms flood my thoughts. I close my eyes and see wild waves breaking over the Gloucester sea wall. The road to Essex deep in saltwater during a full moon, high tide atmospheric rant. The near-hurricane-force wind holding me steady as I lean sharply into it, while rain pummels my face, soaks my hair, and drenches me to the skin. Exciting. Mother Nature having a snit.

The ringing phone pulls me from my reverie. I dash for the kitchen.

"Hello?" All I hear is a man's choked and garbled voice. I can't make out what he is saying or identify the strange gulping sound he's making. Is this an obscene phone call? Then I realize the voice belongs to my brother.

"Ellyn ..." is all he can get out.

"Russell?" I'm not sure he even hears me. Is he having a heart attack? Why is he calling me and not 911? "Are you okay? What's going on?"

"It's RT." His voice is sharp, its pitch unnaturally high. He's crying. No, this is deeper than crying. He's having some sort of crisis.

"RT's been shot."

A familiar shiver runs through my body as I stand at my kitchen counter. My legs give way, and I sit heavily on one of the nearby stools. My mind silently screams NO!, but I hold myself together for my brother's sake.

"RT's been shot? What happened? Was there a hunting accident? Is he going to be okay? Where is he now?"

"He's in the hospital. Still alive, but the doctor's say ..." He breaks down completely, as if saying the next words might make them true. "They say ... They say ... He's brain dead."

My nephew, the dear young man who took such good care of me after Rob died. This can't be happening.

"Oh, no!" I'm crying now. "Tell me this isn't real."

"It's real all right. He was in the barn drinking with his friends when Mary and I heard a gunshot." Russell breaks down again. "We ran out to the barn and there he was, lying on the floor in a pool of blood. Nobody knows what happened. Or at least nobody is telling.

"Listen, Mary and I are at the hospital with him, and I don't want to be gone too long. Call Linda for me, will you? That's all I can say right now, but I wanted to tell you because only you know what hell this is."

"I'll call her. I don't know if he can hear you, but tell RT I love him. I love you too."

A sob is all I hear, then a click.

Another Funeral

November 11, 2004   Portland, Oregon

TWO VIBRANT YOUNG MEN, one thirty-five, the other thirty-one, are dead. Two siblings, brother and sister draw together in tragedy, each having lost a son. Eight months ago, I sat at my son's funeral. Now I sit at my nephew's.

As the Air Force chaplain folds the flag and presents it to my sister-in-law, I wonder how she can be so stoic, when I have disintegrated into a heaping mess of hysteria. Then I realize she is numb, still lost in denial, unable to accept the reality that her son, her only child, her best friend is gone. My brother's eyes are wide, but vacant and hollow. He looks innocent and vulnerable.

The church is packed. Their home afterwards is packed. RT's closest friends linger after everyone else has paid their respects and gone home. It's dark now, and two of them walk outside. I watch through the window as they build a campfire in the open space near the woods, where they all regularly gathered on weekends during the summer to drink, sing, and carry on. They bring chairs from the barn and circle them around the stone ring that keeps the flames in check. When the blaze is strong, they come inside to get Russ and Mary and the remaining grief-stricken friends and family, inviting us to a more intimate tribute to RT.

Ivan pulls out his guitar and strums a few opening cords of Amazing Grace. We join in singing, softly, reverently through our tears. My brother pushes back his chair, pulls out his handkerchief, and walks quickly into the woods where he stops and crumples onto the ground. My sister and I exchange a knowing look. We give him a few minutes to be alone, then go over and encircle him with our love. We exchange no words. We're just siblings bonding in heartbreak.

The Air Force investigation shows no foul play. RT's death is registered as a handgun accident. But there are questions that remain unanswered, big questions. And the Air Force is not answering them.

Who was in the barn? RT's Special Forces friend, who had just returned home from his second tour in Afghanistan only two days ago, his wife, who he had entrusted RT to "watch over" while he was in the Middle East, RT's girlfriend, and another couple.

They were in The Rustic Lounge, a corner in my brother's barn that he converted into a retreat, a hangout complete with a pot-bellied stove, easy chairs, a photo-memory wall, and a refrigerator stocked with Budweiser. They all had been in town drinking and celebrating their friend's return and finished the night here, where they continued to drink to excess.

What happened? My brother told me this story.

"A loud bang woke Mary and me up. I looked at the clock. It was 2 a.m. 'What was that?' Mary asked me, frightened.

'What the hell? That was a gunshot! Who's shooting so damn close to the house and at this hour?' I was instantly awake. 'That came from the direction of the barn. Oh, my god! Oh, no!'

"I jumped out of bed, pulled on jeans and a sweatshirt. Mary grabbed her bathrobe, and we ran toward the door. One of the guys was standing at the kitchen sink and just looked at us as we flew by.

"I saw RT's girlfriend bent over outside the barn, vomiting in the driveway. I ran over to her. 'Don't let Mary go in there!' she yelled, but Mary pushed past her and ran inside.

"There was RT sprawled on the floor, his eyes were open, but they were blank. He was breathing, but just barely. He was lying in a pool of blood that was pouring from a hole in his temple. Mary grabbed him and held him, screaming his name. She tried to revive him, but nothing worked. 'Someone call 911!' she screamed.

"Oh my god, Ellyn, it was unbelievable.

"The police sent a Medi Vac helicopter. We heard it circle a few times, but the fog was too thick, and they couldn't land. When the helicopter flew away, we went absolutely fucking crazy.

"We had to wait for an ambulance to get up here, which seemed like forever. Now I can see that getting him to a hospital sooner wouldn't have made a difference. There was no hope. But at the time, we couldn't believe the helicopter abandoned us.

"Later, I realized when Mary and I ran through the kitchen, the guy who was standing at the sink was washing blood off his hands. Why the hell didn't he come to get us? Why didn't he say anything to us when we ran past? Why didn't he call 911? What the hell was he doing, just standing there washing blood off his hands?"

Russell said he thought there might have been an argument over how RT "watched over" his friend's wife while he was away. She had been unfaithful. Did RT step over the line? Did someone else step over the line? No one said. And who fired the gun?

The next day their friend disappeared. Vanished. Was he arrested? Did he go into hiding? Was the trauma of seeing his friend shot too much for him? Did he flip out and go to a VA hospital? No one knows where he went. No one has heard from him.

"His disappearance was just too much, Ellyn. We'll never know what happened. We'll never know if it was an alcohol-related accident or a murder. If it was murder," Russ closes his eyes and shakes his head as if to get rid of that thought, "did the military cover it up? We'll never know."

Oh, my god. Is that possible? Murder? Cover up? It raises serious questions about our boys who come home from the war zone and go right back into society, especially those who have been trained for and were in active combat. They come home with war-related PTSD. Was this young man too newly home from the battleground, and so deeply enmeshed in his Special Forces hunter-killer mindset that he didn't remember how to handle conflict as a civilian? Why aren't these young men re-programmed to life as civilians before they come home and go out drinking with friends? And go out drinking with friends while carrying guns.

But why would the Air Force cover up a murder? To assuage their role in altering his mind from a normal citizen into a warrior? Did they favor him because he had volunteered for a second tour of duty, and RT had not yet been deployed? Why does no one really know what the hell happened that night?

Too many ugly questions, with no answers.

The only thing we know for sure is RT is dead.

CHAPTER 67

Now I Understand

November 18, 2004 Flying home to Annisquam,
Massachusetts

I HAVE TIME TO reflect as I gaze out the airplane window.
There is so much in my head. Disjointed thoughts about death,
life, and grief swirl around, unanchored. Not all of them make
sense. They leave me feeling as if I'm living in an insane and
surreal world. As if I'm moving through life in a container that
looks like my body as others see me, but I'm really standing
outside of that container. I'm detached from it and watching it
move around and talk as if everything is normal. When it's not.

Two young men who would have carried on the family
names no longer exist. The Peska lineage stops dead with my
nephew's passing. My brother was the only male in the last generation of Peska's, his son RT, the only male in this generation.

My mind flashes to all the material items we amass over
time and what happens to them once we are gone. My daughter
will inherit my house, all my possessions, and my unfinished
business. My brother and sister-in-law are alone, really alone,
the end of the line. What will happen to their twenty-seven
acres on the river and all the man toys (tractor, boats, and other
guy paraphernalia) my brother has gathered in his barn? What

happened to Larry the gold miner's claim, his wreck of a home, his Oreo cookies? And how important are all these things anyway? The truth is, they aren't.

We seem to work so hard to accumulate possessions and for what purpose? What does it mean when our purchases go beyond feeding, clothing, and housing our families in a comfortable and loving way? What is comfortable? Are there limits to what is enough? I once asked a now ex-husband, who seemed to believe his identity came directly from the volume of assets he could acquire, "Will you ever have enough?"

His answer was simple. "No."

Last week I saw a tee shirt that said, "He who dies with the most toys wins." Wins what? My son and my nephew were just getting started in life. They didn't have many toys. Does that mean they lost? No. It should be about who you are when you die, not what you have acquired. Rob and RT had generous hearts, they created joy around them, they loved and were loved in return. These are the "toys" that hold the most value. And if we have to judge, (and why do we?) these are the "toys" that should win.

How has my mind drifted onto this topic? How did I go from death to ranting about material acquisitions? Perhaps it's connected to the unfairness or, better word, the inequality in life. Why does one person find so many opportunities and another finds hardship? Why does one person live a long and healthy life, and two others have theirs cut short?

Another more powerful thought, an explanation perhaps, grabs me as we descend toward Boston's Logan Airport. Two years ago, I was "guided" to reconnect with my brother. Something inside me told me to go to Portland to mend our nineteen years of separation. At the time, I thought it was about relationships, about observing my brother, who is a carbon copy of our dad. I thought it was an opportunity to step back to my childhood, to see how some of my ideas were formed, take a look at the environment that shaped me into who I am today, and then begin to adjust any misdirection. I thought it was also about having a caring big brother for the first time. That was part of it. But only the important beginning.

Eight months ago, I had another aha. I was guided to reconnect with Russell because I desperately needed my brother's love and support after Rob died. And that was true, too. But now, today, here I am, here we both are needing each other in our tragedies. We need each other because no one else we know understands what it's like to lose a child.

I didn't know what was coming. I didn't know I would lose my son. I didn't know my brother would lose his son eight months after I lost Rob. I didn't know the two of us would forge a bond so strong that nothing could ever break it, or that we would need each other in ways we never dreamed possible. Now, when the phone rings and I see his name pop up, but all I hear is, "Ellyn" in a cracked voice, I understand everything. He doesn't have to say a word. "I'm here for you," and, "I know," are all I have to say.

Again, I wonder about this guidance, or intuition, or whatever. Different people have different ways to define where it comes from—God, Allah, The Universe, Higher Power, Spirit, Angels, The Collective Unconscious. I don't really know what to call it or where it comes from, so I won't bother with that. What

I do pay attention to is that it happens, and when it does, we need to pay attention. It's always about something important.

Back in 1985, my husband was driving me to the airport. I was off to London to buy inventory at the street markets for my antiques business. As we parked the car, I had one of those clear guidance moments. "I can't get on that plane," I told him.

"What? What are you talking about?"

"Something just told me to not get on that plane. I'll have to change my ticket."

He was familiar with my quirks, but this made no sense to him. "Ellyn, your plane leaves in two hours. If you change your ticket, you'll lose the great price you got and will have to pay a last minute full fare."

"I don't care. I'm not getting on that plane."

He continued his harangue into the lobby. As I walked up to the ticket counter, an announcement came over the airport PA system. "British Airways flight 6175 to London's Heathrow Airport has been canceled. Please see a ticket agent for assistance."

I smiled as I handed my ticket to the agent. "I need to re-book this flight to London, please. What happened? Why was the flight cancelled?"

"They never tell us. Probably a mechanical," she said. "I can get you on the next flight."

My husband looked at me as if I were magical. I'm not magical. I just paid attention and followed through. Would that plane have crashed if the mechanical had not been discovered? I don't know. I only know I was not to be on it. Just as I knew I had to reconnect with my brother in 2002. And just

as my brother knew not to turn right to the garbage dump in
Vietnam.

CHAPTER 68

Getting Back on Track

January 14, 2005   Email to my sister. San Diego, California

Hi Linda,

I'm in San Diego visiting Ginger. I had a much-needed day to myself yesterday. I went to the beach in La Jolla and walked and walked and cried because this is where I came after Rob died, and the sad and painful memories came flooding back. The next few weeks in California might be tough as this is where all the horrible stuff happened. On the other hand, being here helps me process the pain that's still inside.

I'm glad I had distractions during the holidays. The trip to Washington DC to see "Thoroughly Modern Millie" at the Kennedy Center lifted my spirits. It made me want to sing out loud and do the Charleston (remember how Dad would stop whatever he was doing and launch into a Roaring Twenties dance step featuring his hands crossing back and forth over his knees?) The high emotions that surface around Christmas and New Year's would have been too much to face otherwise.

Yesterday I was so tired and so down, I thought I should go on antidepressants (and that's really saying something because you know how much we all hate pills). I was worried about myself because I was seriously thinking, "What is there in my life to live for?" This scared the heck out of me. I know you know what that's like. Thankfully, I thought about Shannon and snapped out of it.

After my walk, I came back to Ginger's house, plopped in my favorite sunroom, and read the magazine she left for me. The main articles were by Dr. Herb Benson who heads the Mind/Body Clinic (that's where I first got certified as a stress management trainer so many years ago and worked for him, teaching the corporate world how to relax.) The articles reminded me of all the good things meditating and being in the present do for me. So, I did some relaxation techniques right there in the sunroom, which helped bring me back up to a more normal level. I feel much better, don't need the meds and am trying to move toward that more healthful way of living I used to have before Rob got sick and RT died.

What a wild ride I've been on. I'm ready to get back into a more positive mode. I feel the crazy stuff is over, and now I can move forward. It will take some time. I don't think I'll ever get fully back to the old me. Because of what happened, the new me is emerging as a very different person. It almost feels as if my soul has left and there's a new one in my body. Did you feel that way after Charlie died? That you had changed so much that it might not really be you? Or does losing someone you love provide such a different perspective on life that everything that was familiar now feels foreign? That values you thought were so important, really aren't?

I talked with Russell yesterday. He and Mary were on their way to the Oregon coast for a couple days. They seem to be functioning, considering what they've been through.

I'll call you Saturday when I'm on the train to LA. I hope Amtrak is running—the tracks along the way were buried in a mudslide last week and promise to be back on track (ha ha) by Friday night.

I love you, Ellyn

CHAPTER 69

Starting Anew

February 2005   Annisquam, Massachusetts

I RETURN TO ANNISQUAM from San Diego, determined to leave Massachusetts, leave the winter, leave this horrific year behind. A fresh start in San Diego feels like the right thing to do. I've always hated the bone-chilling cold of winter. I envied Rob when he chose the University of Southern California for college, then settled in LA after graduation. How ironic that I was here in Massachusetts, freezing my buns off, when he was there, doing the backstroke in the USC pool. And, now that he's gone, I've decided to move to California. I wish I had made the move earlier. This is just another in a long line of wishes, things I would have done differently had I only known he was going to die so young.

So, California here I come.

Now I have to find a place to live. Ginger, who has been watching over me, solves the problem. "You can move into my guest room. Stay as long as you want to or need to."

I placed a "Furnished House for Rent" ad in the *Gloucester Times* that ran Saturday and Sunday. Instantly, a family of three with a cockatiel responded. They can't wait to move in.

When change comes, and it's right, it comes quickly. Suddenly, I'm moving to San Diego. I pack my personal belongings. The wintry boxes will go to a storage unit in Gloucester, the rest I will ship to my new home in a gentler climate. It feels wonderful to leave the heavy stuff behind.

My kitchen phone rings as I'm wrapping my china plates in yesterday's Sunday *Boston Globe/Help Wanted* section. I rinse the newsprint off my fingers and answer. "Hello?"

"Is this Ellyn Wolfe?"

"Yes. Who is this?"

"This is Mr. B at the Massachusetts Office of Labor and Workforce Development. Our department has been working with your former employer since their merger last March. Because such a large number of employees, over fifteen hundred, were laid off in Boston, we are required to follow up with those who have not yet gone back to work. Have you found another job?"

"Not yet."

"Have you looked?"

"Yes, I've made quite a few applications and had few interviews, but nothing came of them, nor any of my other inquiries."

"Well, I have some good news for you. Your former employer was required to set aside a certain amount of money for retraining those who haven't found jobs, and our department is partnering with them to assist. Since you have not found a position, we would like to offer you a grant for retraining. With this grant, you can go back to school or find a program that will broaden your skill set and open new career pathways."

"Really? That sounds great. Can you be more specific about the kind of class or training program? What classes does the Department offer?"

"I'm talking about going to a university or to private specialized classes. Basically, you have to find a curriculum that will provide new skills, something that will make you more hirable. You do the legwork. I'll email a list of criteria, but it's pretty open-ended. We provide a full grant."

I go silent. Is this for real? A grant to go back to school? I'm almost afraid to respond, to say "yes" and "thank you" in case it suddenly vanishes, leaving me empty again.

"Hello? Are you there?" he asks.

"I'm here. I'm kind of in shock and am trying to take this in. This is so generous." I pause again, wondering if there is a catch. "What do I have to do? How many others are getting this benefit?"

"There are a few others, but most of your former co-workers have found jobs already. There is nothing you need do other than fill out a little paperwork. As soon as you identify a program, we will pay for it directly."

Does this mark the end of *annus horribilis*? This is a true gift, falling out of the sky and right into my lap.

I immediately look at the Harvard Business School's Executive Programs, but they all require me to be in Cambridge for a good part of the year, and I'm on a plane to San Diego in a little over a month. After a week of searching, I find it—a one year "Evidence-Based Life Coach" master's program at Fielding Graduate University, based in Santa Barbara. It starts in September, and it's a combination of online, weekly teleconferencing, and face-to-face learning. I'm free to go to San Diego, try to find a job there, and get another master's at the same time.

These new additions to my life, relocating to San Diego and learning a new skill, give me purpose, give me hope, and carry me forward.

June 2005   Annisquam

I SHIP MY CAR packed to the roof with clothing and necessities, get on a plane, and settle into my new life in San Diego. Two weeks later, I'm looking at Saturday night theater listings when I notice a Jobbing.com ad for a Human Resources Director at the San Diego Convention Center. I shoot them a resume online that includes the Life Coach info. They call the next day to set up an interview. Suddenly I'm employed. But this is too easy. I'm waiting for the other shoe to drop. It never does. I love working here and studying to be a Life Coach is one of the best things I've ever done.

PART VI

CALIFORNIA

CHAPTER 70

Spirit

November 29, 2010   Five years later, my new house. Tierras-
anta, California

IT'S THE END OF the day on Saturday. I'm tired, so I'm doing mindless work—pulling towels out of the laundry basket at my feet, folding, then tucking them onto the shelves in the linen closet. Their neat corners line up military style. I like seeing this kind of order. It balances out the chaos of my life, plus it makes the small cabinet seem a little larger. The hallway where I'm standing is narrow, only a few feet between the cupboard where I'm working and the upstairs banister.

Two towels left. I match the edges of a fluffy white bath sheet and double them over to meet their opposite side. I stop mid-fold. I sense something is different, not normal. The back of my neck prickles. The sensation shoots down my arms, which erupt in goose bumps. The hairs on my arms stand on end. Someone is behind me.

A thousand thoughts race through my mind as fear grips me. I whip around and see a young man leaning against the banister. His arms fold across his chest, his legs cross casually at the ankles. He's wearing jeans and a striped tee shirt, sneakers on his feet. His shoulders are broad like a swimmer's.

But there is something very strange. The colors I see on him and around him are muted, more like sepia tones and—he doesn't have a head!

"Ahhh!" With my shout, he disappears. Evaporates. Vanishes. But I know he was there. And I know it was Rob. The posture is exactly how he used to stand in the kitchen on Masconomo Street, leaning against the counter while I made dinner, talking about swim practice or his day at Manchester-by-the-Sea High. It was comfortable and relaxed. And that's the same feeling I have now. I'm not frightened. I'm peaceful, completely calm with a warm sensation of deep love spreading within me.

A more composed, "Ohhh" escapes with my exhale. This was not an attack, but a gift. It's Rob's second attempt to answer my request before he died, "Please Rob, when you get to the other side, find a way to let me know you're okay." The first was Buzz buzz, Mr. Bumblebee.

I drop the towel back into the basket and stand motionless, staring at the empty space where he was. I'm smiling. I'm happy. He was here. He is here. I simply can't see him when my mind is in everyday awake mode. But when I was "mindless" and on "auto-pilot" folding towels, I must have entered an alpha state, when the body and mind are relaxed and brain waves move into that place between sleeping and waking, the peaceful mental state also brought on by meditation.

Almost six years have passed since he died. This encounter is just what I need to refresh my belief that there is a different kind of life after death, and Rob's spirit, his energy, is still around. I didn't know what to believe after he died. My faith died with him. I felt confused and lost. My only awareness was the ache from a large hole in my heart and deep emptiness. But this experience changes me. This profound visit leaves me feeling bathed in love and filled with joy. I'm lifted up.

Usually when something out of the ordinary happens, I'm eager to share it, to recount every detail. This is different. I don't want to see or talk with anyone. This is only for me, from Rob, and I want to be quiet and take it in. I stay in the upstairs hallway, infused with wonder at this contact from beyond, sit gently on the carpet, stretch my legs out in front of me, and lean against the door frame. My eyes close, my breath is slow and steady, a smile lights up my face. I want to hold onto this sense of joy and peace as long as I can.

A question pops up. Why didn't he have his head? Then I remember something and laugh.

In the summer of 2006, I was walking around the 1870's gold rush mountain town, Julian, California, after enjoying a slice of the area's renowned apple pie. I strolled past an unusual dark brown shingled structure, a wooden tower with windows and door painted a faded teal green. Several signs were nailed around the door. One identified its past as the "Historic Water Tower." "Mind*Body*Spirit*Balance" identified its current inhabitant, a psychic medium, who offered "Channeled Readings," "Reiki and Qigong Healings," and "Spiritual and Meditation Classes." My kind of place.

Two colorful Adirondack chairs framed the entrance. A clipboard with a sign-up sheet and a pencil dangling from an attached string sat on a green table near the sidewalk. FIRST NAME and ONE HOUR/HALF HOUR were printed next to a list of available times. Only one time slot was open. I picked up the menu of services from the table. Prices were reasonable. I had time. She had time. I signed up.

"Hi, I'm Linda," she said as she tucked a cassette into a recorder. I scanned the cozy room quickly as I settled into my chair across the table from her. I responded with, "Hi, I'm Ellyn," and nothing more, not wanting to give anything away, a test to see if she was for real. She closed her eyes then told me about an older man, with pink cheeks and white hair in a flat-top cut, who passed away not too long ago. I felt confused and disappointed. This wasn't even close to what Rob looked like. I listened as she continued.

"He's referring to the letter you wrote to him before he died and wants you to know he kept it at his bedside."

"That's my former father-in-law!" I said completely surprised.

"He wants to thank you for ..." and she delivered a private message to me, which left me in tears and convinced she was the real thing.

"I have a young man here who has a tremendous sense of humor—and a great smile," she said. She told me things she could not have known, but Rob did, like how I'm a crazy driver. "You're driving too fast! Slow down and pay attention to the road!" he warned me through this woman who sees and hears what most of us can't. "Please, Mom. You don't need to be here before your time." He knows I have a heavy foot, and I apply lipstick, blush and mascara while driving, rummage through my purse for peppermints, and (this is by far the worst) I read my notes for the presentation I'm going to give that day. Linda finished delivering his messages, then asked me, "Do you have any questions for him?"

"I know people who awakened in the middle of the night and saw a relative who had died standing at the foot of their bed," I told her. "Please ask him if he's going to come visit me."

She closed her eyes and was silent for a moment. Then she laughed and opened her eyes. "He says, 'Mom, do you know how hard it is to materialize?'"

This reading is what I remember as I sit on the floor by the linen closet after seeing Rob's spirit minus his head. I imagine him so eager to get the materialization process down and so excited when he figures out 90% of it, that he decides to go for it—without his head. I nod in understanding and laugh out loud because it's so much like him.

CHAPTER 71

Ten Years

March 4, 2014   My retirement house. Hemet, California

THE PHOTO MONTAGE I'M building for my living room wall lies on the carpet like stepping stones across a pond. Faces smile back at me. The arranging process is slow as I drift off into reverie, reliving moments captured on film. There's one of Shannon and me hugging each other on the prow of a cruise ship in Alaska's Tracy Arm Fjord, hair matted, multiple layers of clothing soaked through to our skin with freezing rain, grins showing how thrilled we are with each other and the majesty of our surroundings.

There's another of Rob he called, "Holding the Whole World in My Hands." The world is George Lucas' mansion in the background, resting on Rob's hands in the foreground. I become lost, listening in my mind to the stories Rob told about how he and his film crew were chosen to use the state-of-the-art sound studio at Mr. Lucas' Skywalker Ranch for their Indie film, *North Beach*, and how awesome it was when Mr. Lucas invited them to watch a football game with him.

The photos of Rob go only so far in time. They stop in 2004, right after his thirty-fifth birthday.

Exactly ten years ago tonight, he left this world for parts unknown to the living. I think of ten years without him as a milestone, but not sure why. Each year March 4 is a milestone in itself. One more year without his smile, his wacky humor, his sensitivity. One more year without me smiling when I hear his cheery "Hi Mom!" greeting. He left a voicemail on my cell phone while he was getting chemo. The "Hi Mom" is there, but with a tinge of sadness and fatigue. I kept this voicemail for months after he passed away. Too many times, as I opened my phone, his voice popped up with, "Hi Mom." The repeated shock was too much. I had to remove it and save it elsewhere. (The phone company made a recording for me.)

I'm fortunate he was an actor. He left a box of photos, videotapes of TV programs he was in, and audiotapes as lead singer in his band IRATIK. I can see him and hear him whenever I want. I'm grateful for that, as many parents are left with only a few old photos.

Is it easier after ten years? In many ways it is. It's rare now that I see something special and think, "Rob would love this. I'm going to call him." In the early years it happened all the time, then the pain of realization would grip me, and my heart would ache. I still cry from time to time, but rarely. I'm crying as I write this. The reality is the pain never fully goes away. It simply hunkers down in a dark recess in my brain. On the rare occasion when it gets triggered and rises to the surface, I find its bite lacks teeth. Now I mainly remember the everyday Rob—the simple things, the good times, the love. It is easier now. I'm out of the habit of expecting him to be here.

This morning I posted a remembrance photo of Rob at Skywalker Ranch on Facebook. I so appreciate the support that flows in from friends. It helps, yet when I look at his photo and see his vibrancy and his love of life, I can't help but wonder what his life would have been like had he lived. In my mind he will be forever young.

A few days after Rob died, a drunk passed me on the sidewalk. Filthy clothes hung on his emaciated, smelly body. Wine-fueled saliva sputtered from his mouth as he swore bitterly at no one in particular. Anger and disgust consumed me. Why Rob and not him? Rob had so much to offer. He loved life. That sidewalk wino ….

I feel guilty for judging him without knowing his story, without knowing what happened to him. A few days after the wino encounter, I was out walking. Someone smiled at me, but I was so consumed with grief and so detached, I rudely stared at her and walked past. She looked offended. She had no idea I was tortured inside. It made me think about how I responded to the wino and about those who called Rob a druggie when he collapsed in pain after the Chris Rock concert. We don't know what's happening inside others. Let empathy replace judgment.

I've mellowed over time and have come to look at life from a higher perspective. I realize there is no order in life. Children predecease their parents, and there is no "deserving" to be here because one person is better educated or nicer than another human being who has had hard times. I venture back and forth from believing we all have a predestined time to leave the planet, and believing our departure is more technical, a result of the genetic draw. Spirituality vs. Science. Who really knows?

I thought I knew where he went when he left his body during the comas. I thought prayers would be answered, requests for miracles granted. My spiritual teachings gave me what I thought was a sound base. Until he died. Then I realized I knew nothing, and prayers were empty wishes for help from the helpless. Where was the miracle that pulled Rob from the clutches of death in the eleventh hour? I believed right up until he exhaled his last breath there would be a miracle, that all the prayers from all the people we knew around the earth would be heard and answered. Why are miracles selective? How do people hold on to their faith when tragedy like this happens? When faith is gone, the emptiness is vast.

Existential questions haunted me for years. Why? Why? Why? They're there still, but I'm more pragmatic now and respond with a simple, "I don't know," then move on.

I was angry. Kubler-Ross says this is a normal stage of grief, and I know professionally that anger is a coverup for powerful emotions, a way to appear in control when you know you are not. Ten years seems like a long time. It also seems like yesterday. The good news is, I'm not angry anymore. The anger has been replaced with gratefulness. I'm grateful he was part of my life for the thirty-five years he was alive.

CHAPTER 72

Time Heals

March 4, 2018   Hemet, California. Writing the last chapter of this book.

THE PHOTO MONTAGE HAS been on my wall for four years now. Rob and Shannon grace the center, our family radiates out around them. Each picture reminds me of a happy time when smiles came easily.

The two youngest men from this family have passed on, my son and my nephew, but their love, their spirit, and their youthful energy are what I remember and what I carry with me. The horror has all but disappeared.

I think about the hit of intuition that moved me to reconnect with my brother so long ago, not understanding at the time what was ahead of us, what was ahead for our sons. I'm grateful we developed a relationship so we could be there to help each other. Our bond of mutual compassion remains strong after all these years. Nothing will ever break it. It's a gift out of tragedy.

The hospice nurse's comments about grief come to mind, especially in those increasingly rare moments when an event or a memory triggers my emotions. She said time heals, but grief lingers and never goes away entirely. She was right. There will always be a hole in my heart, a piece of me that is missing. But for the most part, time has healed me, just as it's healing my brother and his wife. I look forward to each day with calm instead of fear, acceptance instead of denial, and peace instead of anger.

I still seek distractions, but they're motivated now by curiosity, a desire to learn, or seeking fun rather than avoidance. Loss has intensified my appreciation for life, for its beauty and for its fragility. And I know how important it is to seize opportunities when they present and not linger, thinking mistakenly they will always be there.

One of my biggest lessons is to appreciate and love the people around me while I have them. Death is one of those things I thought would happen in the distant future, not now. But when it stepped boldly into my life, it jolted me awake to its reality. We all are destined to die and not necessarily in old age after our parents.

There is still so much I don't understand about life and death and most likely never will. I do know time heals. And I know focusing on the positives each day has allowed joy to come back into my life. There is so much around me for which I am grateful, so much more than just the color blue.

•   THE END   •

ACKNOWLEDGMENTS

THANKS TO THE WEDNESDAY morning writing group who listened to my first chapter and encouraged me to keep going. And to The Choir Writers who gather at my dining room table to share ideas and inspiration. Beta readers Kathryn Kay, JoLynne Buehring, Sandy Schuster-Hubbard, Michelle Bassett, Jane Holland, Dr. Jim VanDolah, and my sister, Linda Skea, offered valuable insights.

I AM GRATEFUL FOR my daughter, Shannon Mulloy, and daughter-in-law, Angel Anderson, who loved me and cried with me throughout this long and arduous writing journey.

HEARTFELT THANKS TO GINGER Gainer who helped me forge a new beginning and has been there for me ever since. And to Kathryn Kay, founder of *A Writer Within*, for her friendship and support from beginning to end.

I AM INDEBTED TO Dr. Janine Bembechat, Harvard professor, who probably has no idea she instilled courage in me so many years ago when she said, "You must go on."

DEEP GRATITUDE GOES TO The Core Three—Rich Speight Jr., JT Guerin, and Rob Boltin—Rob's best friends, for their tireless support as they tended to his every need from the minute he was diagnosed to his farewell celebration of life.

ABOUT THE AUTHOR

ELLYN WOLFE HOLDS UNDERGRADUATE and master's degrees in Psychology from Harvard. As a Life Coach, stress management specialist, author, and editor, Ellyn is dedicated to supporting others as they face life's challenges.